Valuing Intellectual Property in Japan, Britain and the United States

As over half the assets of many major companies are now intangible assets, there is an increasing need to assess more accurately the value of intellectual property (IP) from a wider interdisciplinary perspective. Re-evaluating risk and understanding the true value of intellectual property is a major problem, particularly important for business practitioners, including business analysts and investors, venture capitalists, accountants, insurance experts, intellectual property lawyers and also for those who hold intellectual property assets, such as media, publishing and pharmaceutical companies, and universities and other research bodies. Written by the foremost authorities in the field from Britain, Japan and the US, this book considers the latest developments and puts forward much new thinking. The book includes thorough coverage of developments in Japan, which is reviewing the value of IP at a much quicker pace than any other country and is registering ever-increasing numbers of patents in the course of inventing its way out of economic inertia.

Ruth Taplin is Director of the Centre for Japanese and East Asian Studies, Editor of the *Journal of Interdisciplinary Economics* and Research Fellow, Birkbeck College, University of London and the University of Leicester. She is the author/editor of nine books and has written special reports on East Asia for *The Times* for eight years.

Valuing Intellectual Property in Japan, Britain and the United States

Edited by Ruth Taplin

RoutledgeCurzon
Taylor & Francis Group

LONDON AND NEW YORK

First published 2004
by RoutledgeCurzon
11 New Fetter Lane, London EC4P 4EE

Simultaneously published in the USA and Canada
by RoutledgeCurzon
29 West 35th Street, New York, NY 10001

RoutledgeCurzon is an imprint of the Taylor & Francis Group

© 2004 Editorial matter and selection, Ruth Taplin;
individual chapters, the contributors

Typeset in Times New Roman by
Florence Production Ltd, Stoodleigh, Devon
Printed and bound in Great Britain by
MPG Books, Bodmin, Cornwall

British Library Cataloguing in Publication Data
A catalogue record for this book is available from the
British Library

Library of Congress Cataloging in Publication Data
A catalog record for this book has been requested

ISBN 0–415–34112–4

Contents

Contributors

Dr Tomoyuki Hisa is Assistant Professor at the University of Tokyo, RCAST, working under Prof. Katsuya Tamai. Dr Hisa specialises in medicine and IP. His Ph.D. is from Osaka City University and his MD degree is from Wakayama Medical College. He has won a number of awards for his work including the On the Spot Award from the National Cancer Institute, US.

Matthew R. Hogg LLB (Hons), LLM is a Technical Underwriter at R. J. Kiln and Co. Ltd, a leading managing agent at Lloyd's of London. Matthew is the intellectual property expert at Kiln having a degree in Law and a Masters in Law and Economics from the University of Manchester. Prior to joining Kiln, Matthew worked in London and the US for a multinational insurance broker, specialising in intellectual property.

Takuma Kiso is Senior Economist and Head, Research Department – Public Policy Mizuho Research Institute and contributes articles to a number of specialist magazines dealing with the rise of entrepreneurship in Japan. He contributed a chapter on entrepreneurship to *Exploiting Patent Rights and a New Climate for Innovation in Japan* edited by Ruth Taplin and published by the IPI in 2003.

Ian Lewis is a Director of Miller Insurance Services Ltd, a leading independent insurance broker. He heads the IP Team at Miller which has an unrivalled level of expertise among European insurance brokers. Ian has been advising industry professionals for over 15 years on the suitability and purchase of intellectual property insurance for litigation, liability and loss of revenue exposures.

Prof. Akio Nishizawa is Professor at the Graduate School of Economics and Management and Director of the New Industry Creation Hatchery Centre at Tohoku University in Sendai, Japan. He is also former Director of the Japanese venture capital organisation JASCO.

Akito Tani is Deputy Director General of JETRO London.

Dr Ruth Taplin is Director, the Centre for Japanese and East Asian Studies, Editor of the *Journal of Interdisciplinary Economics* and Research Fellow, Birkbeck College, University of London and the University of Leicester. She is the author/editor of nine books.

Steve Van Dulken has worked at the British Library since 1974, since 1987 as a patent specialist. He helps to look after the national collection of patents from all around the world, provides training in patent documentation, maintains the library's patent web site and answers awkward questions from enquirers. He is the editor of *Introduction to Patents Information*, now in its fourth edition and of *Inventing the 20th Century*.

Prof. Masako Wakui is an Associate Professor of Osaka City University, Graduate School of Law, who specialises in competition law and writes on IP-related matters.

Terry A. Young is recognised as an international expert in technology transfer, serving on many international advisory committees and boards. He served as President of the 3,200-member Association of University Technology Managers in 2001. He currently divides his time equally between management of technology transfer within the Texas A&M University System and as Editor of the international newsletter, *Innovation Matters*.

Preface

This book addresses the urgent need to re-evaluate risk and understand the true value of intellectual property (IP) in the light of the fact that intangible assets comprise up to 70 per cent of the assets of most major companies today and that profound changes are occurring in Japan concerning IP that have hitherto been unrecorded, especially in the English language. The days of valuing IP as a sole preserve of accountants and lawyers are past – it has become an interdisciplinary exercise involving business practitioners, insurance specialists, financiers, business analysts, venture capitalists and those who hold intellectual property assets such as media, publishing, pharmaceutical, electronics and software companies, and also universities. In this book, experts in their field explain how the interdisciplinary nature of valuing IP is evolving with, for example, the growth in insurance solutions to protect IP. Within this context we look at the growth of IP in different sectors in relation to national agendas in the countries that have most influenced these developments – the US, Britain and Japan. The US recognised the value of IP with the landmark Bayh-Dole amendment that influenced Britain and Japan. The Technical Licensing Organisation (TLO) has spread to Britain and Japan where it has been modified and cross-influenced by the TLO system in the United States which is now bringing forth issues concerning the reappraisal of valuing IP at the point of commercialisation from universities to industry. Japan is privatising all its universities this year to facilitate cooperation with industry in licensing inventions. Unique IP divisions within the universities are being created to promote this process. Japan is inventing its way out of economic inertia as it has done in the past and, in the process, is re-evaluating everything from brand valuation to the role of entrepreneurship through to university–industry relationships, providing lessons that can be learned globally. Japan has been neglected in the literature, especially in relation to patents and IP, despite it being the second largest economy in the world, because of language barriers, its inward looking tendencies, cultural practices and the complexity of the patent system which is demystified in this book. The book also redresses such neglect, especially in

English-language literature by chronicling and explaining all the current changes happening in Japan with respect to IP in a clear fashion and showing the inter-connections between these processes in the US and Britain, all within the interdisciplinary context.

Ruth Taplin, Editor

Acknowledgements

The Editor would like to thank Mike Barrett, Chief Executive and Prof. Peter Mathias, Chairman of the Great Britain Sasakawa Foundation for their vision and generous support in making this book a reality. Ian Lewis, a Director of Miller Insurance and Matthew Hogg, Technical Underwriter, Kiln plc must be thanked for their valuable support on this book, the contribution of their knowledge of how IP is valued in the insurance industry and for the timely sponsorship from their respective companies. JETRO has offered generous support in kindly sponsoring this book. Special thanks to Akito Tani, Deputy Director General, JETRO London Centre and Yutaka Harada, Senior Adviser, Invest Japan, JETRO for their help in shaping this book and for their endurance in attending so many of my presentations on the subject. Akio Nishizawa, Professor of the Graduate School of Economics and Management at Tohoku University and Tony Samuel of PricewaterhouseCoopers must be thanked for their ideas in bringing this project to fruition as well as all of the contributors to this volume.

The book was the result of a Valuing IP seminar that took place at the Patent Office on 25 September 2003, chaired and organised by the Editor. She would like to thank Anthony Murphy, a former Director of the Patent Office, the Great Britain Sasakawa Foundation, JETRO, the Intellectual Property Institute and the Patent Office (with special thanks to Peter Marchant and Sonia Reid) for making this seminar a reality and the foundation of this book.

Some of the figures used have had minor adaptations made to them for the purposes of this book.

1   Introduction

Ruth Taplin

As intellectual property (IP) becomes the main component of business activity, the need to value accurately and protect the IP becomes more compelling. Such valuation used to be the preserve of accountants and lawyers, but the expansion of importance in IP in all sectors of endeavours means that an interdisciplinary approach is required encompassing economists, accountants, lawyers, insurance and other financial service experts and experts in the electronics/IT field. Different sectors are developing their IP at different speeds and levels and according to a variety of aspects of IP. Therefore, valuation has become an even more complex exercise with the number of bisecting variables increasing, which calls for a more sophisticated analysis. Added to this is the cultural assessment of IP and the different stages of valuation. Inevitably, America, the largest economy in the world has been setting the standard which descended into chaos after the dotcom boom failed throwing into disarray all attempts at standardised valuation of IP which, some argue, was caused by misguided attempts at valuation by the financial world. Losing goodwill, which is known commonly as reputation, with respect to intangible assets can have disastrous consequences as shown by the Enron and Arthur Andersen debacles. Ethics, brand names and reputations can be the determinant factors to the buyers of a given product or service as well as other stakeholders in the company such as investors and partners. Japan, the second largest economy, is experiencing a concerted drive to innovate its way out of economic inertia. Government, university and private companies are all working together to reassess IP, its role in encouraging much needed innovation and bringing tens of thousands of unrealised ideas to fruition and licensing. In the first book *Exploiting Patent Rights and a New Climate for Innovation in Japan*,[1] we explain how the new government–industry–university partnership has been encouraging the establishment of Technical Licensing Organisations (TLOs) to promote innovative collaboration between universities and industry[2] through 'Promoting University – Industry Technology Transfer' (the TLO Law). Every issue, from employees' rights to invention, to the applicability of medical practice and products for IP, to the role of entrepreneurship in creating value and the importance of brand valuation, are being reassessed and redefined.

In the US, where university–industry relations with regard to IP have been long established beginning with the all-important Bayh-Dole Act, influencing both Japan and Britain, there are new moves to understand and define the value of the inventions created at universities at the point of commercialisation. Terry Young of Texas A&M University, a recent past President of the Association of University Technology Managers of America, assesses the role of TLOs in closing the gap between University invention and industry need for inventions which is resulting in greater prosperity for the American economy. Within these essential transactions is the need to try to value accurately the resulting IP. This is pioneering work that needs more attention.

The latest developments in English (and European) patent law

The chapter, 'Recent Developments in English Patent Law', written by Anthony Trenton[3] in the book *Exploiting Patent Rights and a New Climate for Innovation in Japan* considered, among other matters, developments in the law of construction of patents in England and anticipated that the approach to construction would be considered by the House of Lords at some stage. As a follow-up to this, it should be noted that the House of Lords has now given leave to appeal in *Kirin-Amgen Inc. and Others v. Hoechst Marion Roussel Limited and Others*, one of the cases reviewed in the chapter, and the appeal is expected to be heard in Summer 2004.

In the coming year or so, a bill amending the UK Patents Act 1977 is also expected. The expected contents of this bill have been outlined in the Government's published conclusions following a consultation on the proposed amendments. The amendments will be of a miscellaneous nature. Among other things, the Act will be amended to provide that patents may be obtained for second or further medical uses of known substances or compositions, without being drafted in the 'Swiss form'. The 'discretion' to allow or disallow amendment of a patent depending on the patentee's conduct will be removed so that the only issues which will arise in amendment proceedings will be whether the amendment is allowable in patent law. Amendments will also be made to the provisions relating to compensation for employees' inventions. In particular, while an employee will still need to show that the employer has received 'outstanding benefit' in order to obtain compensation, the benefit can be derived from the patented invention rather than just the patent itself as was previously the case. Amendments have also been proposed to the threat provisions in the Patents Act (it is a tort in the UK to threaten patent infringement proceedings unless justified). Finally, a procedure will be introduced whereby non-binding opinions can be sought from the Patent Office as to the validity of a patent (where there is a new argument which was not raised during examination) and infringement. The aim of this is to provide a cheap procedure which may avoid the need for full-blown litigation in some cases.

In addition, quite separately, a new streamlined procedure for patent litigation was introduced in England in April 2003. This procedure is available in cases where it is appropriate bearing in mind proportionality, the financial provision of the parties, the complexity of the case and the importance of the case. In contrast with the normal procedure, there will be no disclosure of documents, no experiments, all evidence will be in writing, cross-examination of witnesses will only be permitted on any topic where it is necessary and will be confined to that topic, the duration of the trial will not be more than one day and the date of the trial will be fixed to be around six months after the order for the streamlined procedure is made. It is early days at the moment and it is not clear what impact this will have; however, the patent judges have made it clear that they are keen to ensure that it is used in appropriate cases.

Perhaps the most dramatic changes afoot are still on the horizon. These are the proposals for a (European) Community Patent and the separate proposal for a unified litigation procedure in relation to existing European patents granted under the European Patent Convention. Currently, the position in Europe is that one may either obtain a national patent (from national Patent Offices) or obtain a European patent from the European Patent Office (EPO) under the European Patent Convention. In fact, upon grant, the European patent is a bundle of national patents, granted by the EPO which, subject to post-grant opposition at the EPO, have an independent life from each other after grant. The consequence is that under the current patent system if a patentee wishes to enforce its patents in several jurisdictions (or an alleged infringer defend patent actions in several jurisdictions) this can prove extremely costly, as well as, on occasion, resulting in the somewhat unsatisfactory position whereby courts in different jurisdictions come to different conclusions.

The two proposals on the drawing board are aimed primarily at cutting down on the expense of enforcing patents in multiple jurisdictions in Europe and the uncertainty and inconsistency that can result from multinational litigation. The proposed Community Patent would be a single patent, to be applied for through the EPO, covering the entire European Union. Proceedings would (from 2010) be brought in a single Community Patent Court based in Luxembourg, with an appeal to the Court of First Instance, also in Luxembourg. The court would be able to revoke the patent community-wide, and also order pan-European injunctions. The proposal had, at one stage, seemed to be faltering as agreement could not be reached in relation to jurisdictional issues and the need for translations. However, in March 2003, a common general approach was arrived at whereby the proposal for a Community Patent Court based in Luxembourg was agreed upon and it was agreed that the patent could be filed in one of the three languages of the EPO (English, French or German) and that, upon grant, the claims of the patent would have to be translated into all other languages of the EU. Nevertheless, as well as being likely to be expensive, this latter part of the agreement is leading to further diplomatic difficulties. In particular, at the Competitiveness Council of Ministers in November 2003 agreement could not be reached on the Regulation creating the Community Patent due to disagreements relating to the period for filing the translations of all the claims. Some Member States want the translations to be filed within three months of grant, others want them filed only within two years.

In the meantime, the European Patent Litigation Agreement (EPLA) is well advanced, at least in terms of agreement. The signatories to the agreement would commit themselves to a unified judicial system for dealing with litigation relating to European patents. It envisages the creation of a European Patent Court with a central chamber (the site of which is undecided) and regional chambers, which would have the power to revoke European patents across all designated states which are signatories to the agreement and to rule on infringement. The European patent would thus cease to be a bundle of national patents in the signatory countries but would become akin to a unitary patent. However, while the agreement is well advanced, some states have taken the view that it is incompatible with the Community Patent and that if the Community Patent goes ahead the EPLA should be shelved. While there is, arguably, room for both (particularly as the EPLA may have a useful transitional role during the initial period when a lot of European patents will be in force and not many Community Patents will have been granted), it does seem likely that only one of the proposals will come to fruition. If the Community Patent can overcome the difficulties with translations, then it will be a real prospect, otherwise it seems probable that the EPLA will be the route taken. Either way, it is likely that by the end of the decade we will have a unitary litigation procedure of some kind in Europe. Such a procedure may follow the example set by the current quest to find an International Accounting Standard that will suit the whole of Europe.

The first consideration in assessing the importance of valuing IP and the awareness that IP needs to be protected as the risks and sums involved are becoming greater from different perspectives, is to understand the current swing towards intangible assets, the explosion of interest in valuing IP and the understanding that IP needs protection because the risks and sums involved are becoming greater.

Taisuke Kato, General Manager of Toshiba IP Division Corporate Headquarters in Tokyo, notes how Toshiba understands the importance of placing a value on IP. In developed economies, the migration from manufacturing to services is paralleled by a shift in asset evaluation from physical assets to intangible assets. A well-known example of this, according to Taisuke Kato, is the estimate that two-thirds of the market capital of listed companies in the US can be accounted for by intangible assets, including IP.

While there is increasing discussion on how best to value IP, a unified methodology has yet to emerge. The market value method has its supporters, as it tries to consider not only present royalty streams but also possible future royalty income. However, there remain difficulties in evaluating certain IP assets, particularly future potential. Toshiba is now looking at promotion of a system of relative evaluation that measures their strength in IP against that of their competitors. The consideration here is quantity against quality. Quantity can easily be determined, quality is more problematic, but possible to some extent.

One area where Toshiba has successful IP valuation is the three-tier incentive system that they use to encourage and reward innovation among their researchers and engineers. The first tier is transfer remuneration, under which an inventor can receive as much as 15,000 yen for transferring an idea to Toshiba. Business remuneration is paid if and when that invention is used in product, and licensing remuneration is paid from any licensing income Toshiba might receive for IP. The latter two incentives depend on the market and the extent to which the IP is utilised. Every year, they arrive at a value for productive IP by calculating how much it contributed to actual sales and earned in royalty income. This gave them the basis for open-ended business and licensing remuneration incentives. As a result, there are many cases of engineers receiving IP remuneration of over US$10,000 a year.

Measuring quality, therefore, in terms of value, is another facet of the complexity in valuing IP. This is especially so when intangible assets become the lifeblood of a company and this is also dependent upon the sector.

At an address to Nippon Kyoiku Kaikun, Hitosubashi University, Ian Lewis,[4] notes how the value of IP within the form of intangible assets has become the key driver of business wealth. He compares the list of companies making up the Fortune 500 in 1975 and then 1995 to find that, in just 20 years, a relatively short space of time for companies of that size, 60 per cent of the companies in 1975 have been replaced. Behind this statistic is a dramatic point. In 1975 the market value of these companies accounted for over 60 per cent of that value in terms of tangible assets, which are the physical objects those companies owned and listed in their balance sheets. By 1995, tangible assets accounted for less than 25 per cent, a reduction of 35 per cent, making intangibles comprise more than 75 per cent of the total values of these companies. The bulk of the intangible assets consists of IP, showing that in a relatively short space of time IP has assumed great commercial and economic significance.

Standardisation

Although all businesses own IP, depending on the type it can become the most important asset of the business. The telecommunications, IT and electronic sectors depend on their ability to patent and copyright their products and software. Richard Fry of TTPCom notes that in his business there are several different types of IP that rely on both patent and copyright. The wireless industry is necessarily driven by standards and the most successful ones are open (in fact they are successful because they are open). Having IP in the standard can be very valuable since, by definition, everyone has to use it, the so-called Essential IPR (intellectual property rights). TTPCom has built a business in licensing IP into the wireless industry beyond Essential IP. This IP can take the form of semiconductor device designs, software or even the design of complete terminals.

Some of the IP TTPCom creates can be novel implementations of the standard. This can, for example, be an idea of how to implement a part of the standard more efficiently. Here, there is some creative or technically difficult step that is needed and the resulting IP has value to their customers in terms of allowing them a more competitive product – for example one which can achieve the same performance on cheaper silicon or at lower power. In general, this IP has relatively short life (typically a few years) so these are rarely patented – simply relying on time to market and technical complexity for protection. With 400 million cell phones being manufactured each year the value of this sort of IP can be quite large if it makes significant savings in component costs.

Another form of IP used by TPPCom is simply the timely implementation of the standard and this applies particularly to software. Here, their customers are simply using the companies to enable them to get to market quicker. However, it could be argued that anybody can get access to the standard and implement it, and with many software developers living in relatively low-wage economies the value of this software ought to be quite low. Fry notes that, fortunately for TPPCom, the value of the software is increasingly in its maturity. With GSM networks now migrating to GPRS, EDGE and 3G and being deployed in 200 countries with more than 500 operators using equipment from 10 different vendors, the scope for interoperability problems is huge. Increasingly, real value is becoming attached to this real-world experience and customers are prepared to pay for it to ensure that their terminals do get into the market quickly and reliably. This is an unusual but valuable form of IP.

This latter form of IP is, of course, not so easy to protect by patent – it is normally protected by copyright and of course, since standards and the network implementations are constantly evolving, by being quick to respond to these.

Brand creates tremendous value as witnessed by many well-known named companies such as Coca Cola, Microsoft or Boeing. It is important in all countries, as shown in Chapter 8 of this book, where Akito Tani examines and explains the 140-page METI (Ministry of Economy, Trade and Industry) report that assesses the possibility of an objective valuation for brands.

Tony Samuel of PricewaterhouseCoopers[5] notes that particular problems arise for accountants; financial statements are of limited use to users when considering the value of a company's IP. Only the acquired IP is on the balance sheet, not the internally generated IP.[6] Therefore, if Coca Cola was to acquire Pepsi (an unlikely scenario), it may feasibly have a value for the brand name Pepsi on its balance sheet, but not a value for Coca Cola. The IP is also shown at acquisition cost, not value. Samuel points out that, while the two were arguably the same at the date of acquisition, the relevance of the acquisition price to the value of the IP declines as time passes.

The rise of the Internet, itself, has contributed to the realisation of the value of IP as businesses have seen their brands, and names as well, used without consent as domain names. The medium of the Internet has also allowed others to infringe upon their products and content. This has been exacerbated by different countries changing and amending their IP and a lack of standardisation which, in Chapter 7 by Masako Wakui, Associate Professor, Graduate School of Law, Osaka University, we will see affects the telecommunication electronics sector, patent pools and working with different countries' patent laws. She also brings out this point regarding competition law which can differ from country to country and, in relation to patent pools and standardisation, influences the values of IP.

There are some commonly used approaches to the valuation of IP. Tony Samuel notes that, historically, the valuation of IP in Japan as well as most Western economies has been driven primarily by transactions, accounting and tax/transfer pricing issues. Looking forward, one would expect the need to value IP to become more frequent given the new US accounting standards and the Japanese government's intention to strengthen IP rights. However, a frequent question is why IP is not on the balance sheet. In fact, IP can occasionally be found on the balance sheet, but such 'values' need to be treated with caution. Tony Samuel explains the reason for this:

> There is a fundamental difference between the purpose of the balance sheet and the concepts used in valuation. A balance sheet reports historic costs; the source of funds (shareholders, creditors) and how those funds were spent (acquiring fixed assets, etc.). For this reason, IP will generally only appear on the balance sheet when it has been acquired. It will not appear on the balance sheet (except in unusual circumstances) when it has been generated internally.

Outside the world of accountants and valuers, the methodologies for valuing IP are not widely understood and, as a result, are not widely trusted.

This is not surprising as valuation is the measure of future benefits, which are necessarily subject to future events and therefore uncertainty: it requires judgement. The application of judgement does expose valuation to some cynicism. It follows that the better the inputs to the judgement process, the more robust the outcome. It also follows that it will always be sensible, wherever possible, to use more than one approach to IP valuation in order to cross-check the result.

Within the world of valuers, there are commonly used and robust methodologies which, when applied with suitable knowledge, experience and consistency, will produce results that are both reliable and meaningful in many decision making processes.

In order to value IP, it is necessary to demonstrate that:

• The asset is separately identifiable.
• There is a legal title to the asset that is owned by the organisation and can be transferred. Other intangible assets, such as goodwill, would not satisfy this test. (In the accounting world, goodwill is defined as the difference between the value of a business and the value of its identifiable tangible and intangible assets.)
• The asset is capable of generating cash flows when unbundled from the underlying business and its goodwill. This concept can generally be satisfied for patents, copyright and product trademarks, as they are all capable of generating a separable cash flow through licensing. It is less obvious that it can be satisfied by corporate brand names that attach to an entire business.

Having established that IP is valuable and should be valued the question arises as to how to value it. This area is complex and, like business and property valuations, subjective. However, certain robust methodologies have been developed, some of which are summarised below. Due to the issues of judgement, valuers will often use more than one methodology in each case, with the results cross-checked to ensure a reasonable result. Tony Samuel also recommends consistency of use over time so as to reduce the comparative effect of judgement wherever possible.

The basic premise underlying the value of any asset is that its current value equals the future economic benefits derived from its use, at today's prices. If an asset has no future economic benefit then it has no value. The difficulty is in (1) forecasting future cash flows; (2) estimating what proportion of those future cash flows can be attributed to the asset; and (3) determining an appropriate discount rate to put those cash flows in present-day terms.

The following methods are commonly used in the US, Europe and Japan.[7]

Premium profits

The underlying principle supporting the premium profits method is that a value can be determined by capitalising the additional profits generated by the intangible asset. This approach is often used for brands on the theory that a branded product can be sold for more than an unbranded product. For instance, Coca Cola may be able to charge 50p for a Coke whereas an unbranded cola may only sell for 35p per can. The price difference of 15p can be described as the value of the brand, per can. To value the brand it would be necessary to forecast the number of annual sales of the branded product and multiply this by the price premium (i.e. the 15p). The sum of the discounted annual price premium would be the estimated value of the brand.

It may be that the product cannot sell at a higher price than the non-branded product but, instead, can sell greater volume. The same valuation technique still applies. The future economic benefits will, thus, be the profits attributable to the additional volume generated by the brand. In many cases, branded products will be able to charge a price premium as well as sell greater volumes than the non-branded competitors.

There are problems with the premium pricing method. First, it is difficult to find a non-branded or generic product to compare prices with. Second, prices charged for each product will vary between regions, and will change throughout the year, given promotions and so forth. In addition, it is very difficult and subjective to establish how much the pricing differential can be attributed to the brand and how much relates to other factors (for example, a distribution network).

The relief from royalty method

This method is based upon the amount a hypothetical third party would pay for use of an IP asset or, alternatively, the amount the owner is relieved from paying by virtue of being the owner rather than the licensee. The estimate of how much a hypothetical third party would pay to be able to use, for example, the name Gucci on their products, provides an estimate of the value of the brand name Gucci. This estimate is based on either actual licence agreements, comparable market data or financial analysis. For example, Gucci may actually be charging licensees a royalty for use of the name; if they are not, then names comparable to Gucci may be used to derive benchmarks for reasonable royalty rates. For valuation purposes, the royalty rate is usually expressed as a percentage of sales.

Once a royalty rate has been estimated it is necessary to estimate the life of the asset and the level of annual sales. Multiplying the level of annual sales by royalty rate and summing all years provides an estimate of the future economic benefit. The final step is to bring these projected future cash flows back to today's prices by discounting for the time value of money and the risks associated with achieving those cash flows. This is the most simplistic and most commonly used method for valuing IP. One difficulty with it is the lack of actual, comparable agreements on which to base the hypothetical royalty rate. This problem can be resolved by analysing the profitability of the products in question in order to estimate the royalty that a hypothetical third party would be prepared to pay in order to generate those profits.

Earnings basis

This method focuses on the maintainable profitability attributable to the intangible asset. The profitability of the product that can be attributed to all other factors, such as tangible assets and working capital, is deducted from the total forecast profitability. The profit remaining, by matter of deduction, can then be attributed to intangible assets. For example, if a branded product had expected future profitability of £100 million and the profit attributed to other factors was estimated at £80 million, then the profit attributed to intangible assets is £20 million. This would then be divided between the company's various intangible assets.

To calculate the value of the brand a multiple is applied to the portion of the £20 million of profit attributed to the brand. Therefore, if a multiple of 10 was considered appropriate and, for simplicity, the profit attributed to the brand is the full £20 million, then the value of the brand would be £200 million (20 × 10). The multiple could be determined by the companies P/E ratios, comparable rates used for other companies, or calculated from scratch, possibly based on factors relating to the strength of the brand.

One shortcoming of this approach, according to Tony Samuel, is that it is difficult to objectively attribute a profit element to all of the other factors, such as tangible assets. Second, the profit attributed to the brand will depend on how certain costs are allocated. Third, the calculation of a multiple is highly subjective.

Market transaction comparatives

Another method of valuation is by reference to actual comparable transactions. For example, in 1998 Diageo sold its Bombay Gin and Dewar's Scotch whisky to Bacardi for US$1.9 billion. By analysing the acquisition price as a multiple of current or forecast sales it would be possible to estimate the value of another brand in the same sector. However, comparable transactions are rare and would be of use for a limited time span only.

Cost approach

This is less frequently used as there isn't necessarily a direct link between historic cost and future benefits. It is also used as a reference to replacement cost, however, that does have some relevance. In determining damages, for example, it is relevant to consider the cost of designing around an invention as a means of determining how much a licensee might pay a licensor for a particular technology. Its application is relatively limited; for example, the cost of creating music copyright bears no relationship to the success of the music – similarly, significant sums could be spent on developing a brand that has little or no value.

Protection and enforcement

IP has been in the domain of lawyers for many years, requiring close legal attention for protection and enforcement reasons. The focus on the role of IP in creating value for a company has increased significantly in recent years which, in turn, has led to a wider discussion on the need to value IP and understand the valuation methodologies available. This focus is apparent in all economies and is evidenced in Japan. Tony Samuel expects this focus on IP and on IP valuation to continue as more companies become aware of the need to use valuation principles in the strategic management of IP to improve their future cash flows.

The increased movement towards IP representing the bulk of companies' assets with even newer risks occurring as a result of change in the global business model, as well as the increasing complexity of valuing IP, is leading many IP managers to consider an insurance solution.

Matthew Hogg[8] notes, and expands upon this in his chapter, that in terms of risk there is still the mistaken belief that all IP-associated risks are a business risk that cannot be shared with third parties. Traditionally, business has sought partners to help share the burden of unexpected losses, property, marine and other tangible insurable property items. This is changing with the move towards the majority of assets becoming intangible, with a whole new source of valuation opening up with insurance using IP cover to both protect and develop the value of business IP rights.

Drawing from surveys conducted both by AIRMIC (City of London-based Association of Insurance and Risk Managers) and Aon European Risk Management and Insurance Survey 2002–3, Matthew Hogg points to the most recent fears for business. Not long ago, fire would have been the main cause of concern, but the typical top three greatest risks facing businesses are now more likely to be business interruption, loss of reputation and products liability/tamper/brand protection. The lack of awareness of these needs has been a combination of the insurance industry not facing up to the challenge to provide coverage for these particular areas coupled by the lack of pressure from commerce to encourage such coverage. He further notes that, although AIRMIC has frequently highlighted the new risks to be faced by business, consideration of these threats is often not integral to the function of the risk or insurance manager. Too little attention is given to intangible risks and evidence from the survey shows that only 22 per cent of companies have a formal brand and reputation strategy in place.

Ian Lewis lists and elaborates further, in Chapter 5, on IP exposures that are making businesses begin to seek insurance solutions to both value and protect their IP assets.

Need to enforce[†]

Because of the value and competitive advantage these rights afford, many organisations incur significant costs in registering patents, trademarks and designs and go to extreme lengths to establish their copyright. Unfortunately, some businesses will try to ride on the backs of others by designing products or services as close to the original as possible.

While this may be seen as fair business practice, some companies get too close and infringe the relevant patent, design or trade mark, thereby threatening the value of the right and reducing the return to the owner of the right.

The problem for the owner of the IPR is to stop the infringement. The person who infringes inadvertently will usually stop upon receipt of a Cease and Desist letter from a lawyer, but the determined person who infringes (or those who genuinely believe their product is different) will be much harder to stop. The intellectual property right owner either has to negotiate or litigate to resolve the matter and this will, of course, be costly.

Failure to enforce such rights may be interpreted by others as a sign of weakness and encourage them to infringe as well, thereby compounding the loss in revenue or even threatening the very existence of the owner of the rights.

It is not unheard of for companies to undertake financial searches on small development companies to ascertain their ability to enforce their rights. If the small company appears financially weak, such larger firms may blatantly copy the small firm's products, safe in the knowledge that the small firm cannot afford to litigate. The experience from the UK market is that having good insurance protection, and actively promoting the fact, is a good deterrent to those who contemplate infringement.

Challenges

Unfortunately, infringement is not the only risk facing the intellectual property right owner. A challenge to the validity of the IP can be more devastating and is becoming the favoured tactic of many. If a competitor can remove the 'monopoly position' afforded by the right concerned, they will have an open field to promote the same product or use the process.

[†] Material from this point, until [†] on p. 13 is taken, with minor adaptations, from Chapter 5.

To the IP owner, this would mean the loss of all of their investment in Research & Development, trials or testing, marketing, tooling and so forth, let alone the loss of future sales revenue. These sums can be vast, especially in fields such as biotechnology, pharmaceuticals or petrochemicals where development costs and subsequent profits are high.

There is a common misconception that, once granted, patents and other rights are set in 'tablets of stone'. This is not the case; they are vulnerable to attack on the grounds of invalidity, ownership or title. A competitor can even apply to the courts for a declaration of non-infringement to try to prevent the rights being enforced at a later date. In Europe, as in Japan, opposition proceedings can be brought after grant of the patent by the respective patent office. In Europe this is often used as a negotiating tool to commence licensing discussions.

Infringement defence

Ian Lewis notes that, even despite not holding IPR, a company or an individual can still have an exposure. All businesses are exposed to the risk of infringement of IPR at one time or another. The exposure is increased if the company imports, manufactures, distributes, sells or even offers for sale a product or process. Somebody else's intellectual property rights may protect all or part of the product or process. If an action was brought this can be very costly, especially since if the case is lost the losers may be liable to pay damages based on an account of profits or their lost revenue.[†]

Exploitation agreements

Increasingly companies are exploiting their IP through licence agreements or distributorship agreements, or transferring know-how and trade secrets via confidentiality and secrecy undertakings. These agreements are the tools through which many companies obtain tremendous wealth and control over the use of their technology. Such agreements are often the result of many hours of negotiation and legal wrangling. It is, therefore, important that companies are able to enforce the terms they have agreed or defend their position in the event that another party claims they have breached the conditions of the agreement.

Ian Lewis makes the point that the most common disputes relate to non-payment of royalties, sales made outside of agreed territories or the enforcement of indemnity clauses agreed between the parties.

Every company or business will have their own unique concerns with regard to IP, be it the enforcement of their own rights, the risk of infringement of another person's rights or both. Some may have large reserves to fall back on, others very little. However, the common theme throughout

---

[†] See footnote on facing page.

all of these concerns is the protection of the balance sheet. Many small businesses can be wiped out by an IP dispute – large firms can see dramatic falls in their share price.

Financial implications

The costs incurred in IP litigation are high. Experienced intellectual property lawyers are at a premium and, as a result, IP is one of the most expensive areas of law to litigate. There are dramatic variances in the cost by jurisdiction. It will be no surprise to learn that the US is the most expensive. The average cost of patent litigation in the US is between $1.5 million and $2 million. There are, of course, cases that cost far in excess of this although it is rare that they exceed $10 million.

In the United Kingdom, costs would average between $500,000 and $1,000,000. As in the US, some cases will be in excess of this. There have been actions that have cost in excess of $10 million; however, such litigation is very rare and is usually only encountered by multinational companies.

An example of such high costs would be the high-profile case of *Andreas Pavel v. Sony Corporation* that revolved around the rights affecting the 'Walkman'. If Sony had lost, it would have had a dramatic effect on their profits. In fact, Sony won the case but the costs in the case are reported to be in excess of £2 million. What makes this case more unusual is that Mr Pavel was funded in his action by Legal Aid.

In Japan, best estimates are that costs would be similar to those of the United Kingdom (i.e. around $500,000–$1,000,000).

Interestingly, the cost of litigation in mainland Europe is very unpredictable. In many jurisdictions, action can be finalised for under $50,000 where a summary judgement is made. However, costs can rise to many hundreds of thousands of dollars.

But litigation costs are not the key concerns for many businesses. If a company is found to have infringed the rights of others, it may have to pay damages.

To put the level of awards in the US actions alone into perspective, Ian Lewis notes of the cases that have had awards made by the courts:

   35% have been lower than $500,000
   15% have been between $500,000 and $5,000,000
   30% have been between $5,000,000 and $10,000,000
   20% are above $10,000,000.

Awards in other jurisdictions are not usually so high, but even in the United Kingdom awards of $15 million and $27 million have been handed down by the courts.

The Japanese case

Japan is a particularly interesting case in terms of valuing IP because all the organisations and social structures are changing at different levels and different speeds. Akio Nishizawa,[9] whose slides are in the Appendix, shows how the university–industry relationship in relation to IP is changing based on the American model from the 1980s. His chronicling of changes since the introduction of the TLO is instructive in its detail but also in its depth of explanation of how Japan is becoming, intensively, a patenting society with increasing success. While following the university–industry IP models of America, Japan is creating its own unique developments. One is the soon to be introduced government approved plan to establish intra-university IPR Divisions that solely exist to give advice and support to those in the university who wish to bring their inventions to fruition. MEXT (Ministry of Education, Culture, Sport, Science and Technology) has awarded such IPR Divisions to 34 Japanese universities.[10]

These dramatic developments all began on 9 July 2003, when the National Diet of Japan enacted a new law that changed the legal status of Japanese national universities. Under this new law, all the national universities in Japan, which previously were national institutions without their own legal status, became independent legal entities with their own decision-making systems. This law has taken effect on 1 April 2004. At that time, these universities are expected to be managed as independent, self-standing organisations. The employment status of their faculty and staff will change from national government employees to university employees, a status no longer governmental.

One consequence of this drastic change to the legal status of the Japanese national universities has been many spirited discussions and debates regarding the ownership and management of IPR which will emerge from the research activities of this new system of universities. Previously, IPR resulting from research of national universities normally was owned and managed by the faculty inventor. However, if the research project was funded with a major grant from the Japanese government, or if it required significant and designated facilities, IPR ownership resided with the national government. In the new paradigm, who will own the IPR? Furthermore, how should the IPR be managed for effective technology transfer from the universities to industry and for university spin-off ventures? Recent discussion has been fierce, not only in the universities and their controlling government body, MEXT, but also in industry, and METI, a government agency that assists the university-related TLOs.

In conjunction with the preparation of the new law to change the legal status of the national universities, Akio Nishizawa points out that MEXT recently established several special committees to explore solutions to the questions surrounding IPR management in the new university system. Experts from academia, industry and related fields were nominated and

recruited to serve on these special committees. After significant deliberation, the committees reported to MEXT that there were four major issues
that warranted attention and solution before April 2004:

1   Ownership of IPR resulting from research conducted at former national
    universities.
2   Management infrastructure and protocol to accomplish the transfer of
    the IPR to commercial application for public and economic benefit.
3   Identification of sources of funding for filing, prosecuting and main-
    taining patent applications to protect the IPR.
4   Workforce development, in recognition of the extreme shortage of indi-
    viduals in Japan with expertise and skills in managing IPR resulting
    from university research.

As to IPR ownership, in light of the new independent status of the universities, it would seem logical that ownership of IPR would reside in the
university. Unfortunately, the language of the new law is not clear or
precise, stating that the former national universities can own the IPR 'in
principle' after April 2004. Thus, according to Akio Nishizawa, it appears
that the Diet left the former resolution of the IPR ownership question to
be determined by MEXT and the universities in policy decisions.

Regarding the management of infrastructure, MEXT proposed that each
former national university establish an internal IPR division or department
that would maintain direct and close working relationships with existing
TLOs at other institutions for effective transfer of research results to
commercial application. Furthermore, MEXT allocated a budget of 2.4
billion yen per annum for the first five years to assist in the establishment
and operation of IPR divisions within selected universities.

Tomoyuki Hisa argues, in Chapter 4, that certain sectors in Japan are subject to a different form of IP valuation. Medicine is such an area, in which
society determines the value of IP and it is linked to issues of humanity
rather than strictly monetary ones. He reviews the current court decisions
that uphold this thesis distinguishing between industrially valuable medicines and medical practices/medical treatment and human rights.[11]

Akito Tani,[12] in Chapter 8, not only describes the intensive re-evaluation
of brand that is occurring but explains the basis of the official governmental strategy for turning Japan into a nation built on IP. This was
emphasised strongly in Prime Minister Koizumi's policy speech of
February 2002, and the *Intellectual Property Policy Outline* of July 2002
published by the IP Strategy Committee in March 2002. This provides our
readers with a sound understanding of how the drive to innovate through
IP has become a national movement in Japan, initiated from the top and
implemented throughout the society.

With Prime Minister Koizumi's re-election in early November 2003, the
political mandate for him to continue to carry out these reforms has been

given by the electorate. This means that, following the manner of Japanese decision-making in which consensus is achieved by preparing the roots of an organisation through the processes of *uchiawase* and *nemawashi*, the Japanese population all supports the IP policies outlined.[13] This process of decision-making means that decisions are made between employers and employees from both the top down and bottom up. Although top managers sometimes float ideas, they are discussed and analysed throughout the company and then suggested for ratification at the top (the *ringi* system) once discussion has taken place at all company levels. The final formal approval is called *ringi* and occurs when the document decided upon is passed from office to office for responsible officials to stamp with their seals. After this, the decision is sent down from the top and implemented quickly and efficiently because all those in the company have already been prepared for the decision. This type of consensus decision-making was demonstrated nationally on 18 April 2003 when an invention day was carried out throughout Japan and all the population was acquainted with the importance of inventing and IP. In daily news such activity was given prominence and the head of the lawyers association stressed how important IP is and explained in newspaper articles how lawyers will give emphasis to invention and IP. As shown in Akio Nishizawa's slides in the Appendix, a whole process of reorganising throughout industry, government and university is a nationwide exercise in consensus-based decision-making according to the principles of *nemawashi* and *uchiawase*.

A good deal more information and background is provided in this book with regard to Japan, as at present next to the US and increasingly the UK, Japan is the country in the forefront globally in its concerted efforts to develop IP. There is also a dearth of literature in English explaining these activities. Few scholars and even fewer business people have made sufficient efforts, or been able, to take on the onerous task of overcoming the language and cultural barriers to understanding the complexity of change in Japan. This is amply demonstrated in Chapter 9 of this book by Steve Van Dulken,[14] of the British Library who explains about the ways of using Japanese patent publications for information. It is an abridged, revised version of the chapter from the British Library's *Introduction to Patents Information* that Van Dulken edits. He explains Japanese numeration and document codes that have only become moderately more Westernised in very recent years. Also explained are the patenting procedure, specifications and abstracts coupled with samples such as the Patent Abstracts of Japan documentation.

Changes in Japan in the IP area continue to move rapidly forward, with some recommending a ninth independent High Court to be created solely to deal with infringement cases. In the end a compromise solution has been created of an 'Intellectual Property High Court' within the Tokyo High Court, which should be established in April 2005. In the case of patent attorneys, 533 patent attorneys (*bendishi*) have passed an examination that complies with a recent law allowing patent attorneys to jointly and equally represent clients with attorneys at law (*bengoshi*). The Japan Patent Attorneys Association President Sumiko Shimosaka noted at a recent IP symposium that patent attorneys are now set to assume an important role in creating, protecting and utilising IP (*Japan Times*, 24 February 2004).

Finally, Professor Katsuya Tamai, of RCAST, University of Tokyo, expert on employees rights to compensation (who contributed a chapter on this topic to the first book of this series *Exploiting Patent Rights and a New Climate for Innovation in Japan*) appeared on NHK television in early February 2004 explaining the significance of the award of 20 billion yen to inventor Shuji Nakamura by Nichia Corporation. Nakamura was instrumental in the development of a LED semiconductor that glows blue when electricity is passed through it. This invention could net Nichia Corporation 120.8 billion yen in profits through its exclusive ownership rights up to October 2010. The Tokyo District Court calculated that Nichia should pay Nakamura half of the potential profit amounting to 60.43 billion yen, but since Nakamura had asked for 20 billion yen the court ordered Nichia to pay that amount as compensation for his invention. This landmark ruling will not only make corporations acutely aware that they need to adequately compensate their inventors or risk losing talented researchers, but also encourage a Patent Law to be created that will force corporations and employers to set the value of patents for contractual purposes. The art of valuing IP is entering its most crucial stage.

Notes

1 Published 2003 by the Intellectual Property Institute, by Dr Ruth Taplin.
2 See Akio Nishizawa 'From tech-transfer to university start-ups. How Japanese universities are responding to new policy change', in ibid. pp. 39–55.
3 See Anthony Trenton 'Recent developments in English patent law', ibid. pp. 87–96. Mr Anthony Trenton is a Solicitor Advocate at Taylor Wessing, specialising in patent law. He has been involved in major UK patent litigation including the most recent proceedings between *Kirin Amgen Inc. and Others v. Hoechst Marion Roussel and Transkaryotic Therapies*.
4 Ian Lewis, Director, Miller Insurance on 29 September 2000.
5 Tony Samuel leads the Intellectual Property and Licensing Disputes practice at PricewaterhouseCoopers in London. He provides expert witness evidence in IP disputes on financial issues, including the value of IP, damages arising from infringement and reasonable royalty rates. He also leads teams in the enforcement of licence terms and advises companies on how to manage their IP and licence portfolios.
6 Internally generated intangible assets can be included on the balance sheet but only when it has a readily ascertainable market value that very few intangibles possess.
7 The METI report identifies Cost, Market and Income approaches to brand valuation and alternatives. The METI report is explained by Akito Tani in Chapter 8. Other methods are also applied, depending on the nature of the IP and the purpose of the valuation.
8 Kiln plc. From *AIRMIC Express*, June 2003.

9 Akio Nishizawa is Professor at the Graduate School of Economics and Management and Director of the New Industry Creation Hatchery Centre at Tohoku University in Sendai, Japan. He is also former Director of the Japanese venture capital organisation JASCO. This material is taken from *Innovation Matters*, 15 August 2003, Volume 1, Issue 6 with the kind permission of the editor, Terry Young of Texas A&M University, and Akio Nishizawa.

10 These are listed among Professor Nishizawa's slides in the Appendix.

11 Tomoyuki Hisa is Associate Professor at RCAST, University of Tokyo and a medical doctor specialising in dermatology.

12 Akito Tani is Deputy Director General JETRO London Centre.

13 These refer to gardening terms which have to do with preparing the roots of the tree before it can be moved successfully. With regard to an organisation, decisions are made by ideas being discussed both vertically and horizontally at all levels. This prepares everyone to implement the decision and express concerns or ask questions about the decision. Once agreed and the directive is issued from the top everyone is prepared for action. See, for further elaboration, Ruth Taplin *Decision-Making and Japan – A Study of Corporate Japanese Decision-Making and its Relevance to Western Companies* (Folkestone: Japan Library, 1995).

14 Steve Van Dulken has worked at the British Library since 1987 as a patent specialist. He is editor of *Introduction to Patents Information* (London: British Library, 2002), now in its fourth edition, and of *Inventing the 20th Century* (London: British Library, 2000).

2 Technology transfer from US universities

The need to value IP at the point of commercialisation

Terry A. Young[1]

In this chapter we present a summary of the history of the birth and growth of university technology transfer in the US which has provided the foundation for understanding the explosion of university research commercialisation occurring in the US today. In addition to exploring the economic impact of this phenomenon, we seek to identify the role of technology transfer in the academic environment in the knowledge-based economy of the twenty-first century. The principles that guided US universities in 2001 remain today and are influencing strongly the emergence of TLOs in Japan. Revisiting the point of commercialisation that occurs at universities, from where a good deal of inventions derive, will assist us in re-evaluating the value of IP.

The term 'intellectual property' scarcely existed in the vocabulary of university researchers in the US even twenty years ago. Universities did not worry about how they communicated with society. Today, intellectual property is a constant part of daily discussion in a research university. This phenomenon reflects a changing relationship of university to society, perhaps something of a revolution, in fact. We will describe the background to those changes, as well as some impacts, and close with some current trends that are now happening in industry, defining the value of IP at the point of commercialisation.

Any discussions of technology transfer start with the fundamental missions of research universities in the US. These are focused upon knowledge, the creation of knowledge through the research, the preservation and dissemination of that knowledge through education and, finally, the transfer of that knowledge to the public through public service and technology transfer. So, we describe a three-fold mission for US academic institutions: 'research, education and service'.

The US economy grew from an agricultural base in the eighteenth and nineteenth centuries, to a manufacturing and industrial base in the twentieth century. Today, the US is entering the knowledge era. The university has an even greater role to play in the twenty-first century. Universities will contribute to this new economy in the training of the leaders for the new industry, and in the training of the skilled workforce. Information technologies, biotechnology, and applied materials will have diverse application in many industries. In achieving its teaching, research and service missions, in the creation and dissemination of knowledge, the university will be a significant contributor to the knowledge-based economy of the future.

In achieving these missions, universities have long engaged in technology transfer, although we might not have identified such activities as technology transfer. First, of course, is the student – 'people embedded technology transfer' – as graduates move into the workforce. The faculty at Texas A&M University prepare papers describing their research results that are published in peer-reviewed journals and are presented in conferences, another form of technology transfer. Daily, there is informal collegial networking between the scientists, facilitated today by the Internet. Research results delivered to the sponsors who fund research at US institutions, and faculty consultation with industry are yet other forms of technology transfer. The sharing of tangible research results and materials has become more important today in biotechnology. In summary, there are many technology transfer activities, which occur as core functions of our universities, without any involvement whatsoever of the TLO.

Niels Reimers, who was the founder of the technology commercialisation effort at Stanford University and directed the programme for 22 years, made a statement that was very profound. He stated, 'Society, having funded much of the university based research, has an expectation that the fruits of that research will improve the human condition.' Likewise, the public – our constituency – expects that the public resources invested in our universities will be managed effectively, with good stewardship.

University technology transfer is a process to move research results to the marketplace for commercial application. For the purpose of this chapter we define technology transfer as follows: 'the process for transfer of university-developed intellectual property rights from the university to the for-profit sector for purposes of commercial application'.

Do we need TLOs?

This definition leads us to the obvious question: why do we establish TLOs? There are five basic reasons. First, technology transfer is needed today to reward, retain and recruit faculty members. It is a very competitive environment in the US today to recruit the best and brightest scientists, as well as to retain them. Today, when scientists visit the campus of Texas A&M University to consider employment, many times they ask for an appointment with technology managers (such as the author) to determine how the university manages IP. Thus, it is important today in the US to have a TLO to serve the needs and expectations of the faculty.

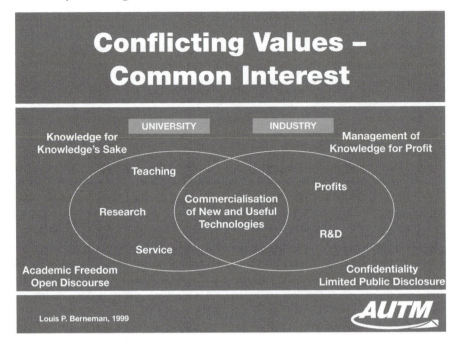

Figure 1

Source: © Louis P. Berneman, 1999. Used by permission.

Second, TLOs are in a position to create closer ties to industry. To understand the process of commercialisation that allows us to value IP it is important to encourage a better and closer relationship between universities and industry. TLOs are critical to establish an effective interface.

Third, TLOs are important to promote economic growth for the region and the nation. Local governments in the US today are looking to the universities as 'engines for economic development'. Through providing new product opportunities to companies, by spinning out new companies and creating new employment opportunities, a valuable contribution is being made to the economic growth of the region and of the nation. This is becoming an even more important role for TLOs in the US today.

Fourth, the TLOs manage a process of commercialising and transferring research results for public good and benefit. Public benefit is the foundational principle for such activities, the primary 'reason for being'. Without TLOs, there would be many goods and services that would never reach the marketplace.

Finally, TLOs exist to generate income for research and education which, perhaps, is the least important reason for creating TLOs. While income for research support is important, TLO-generated income will continue to be

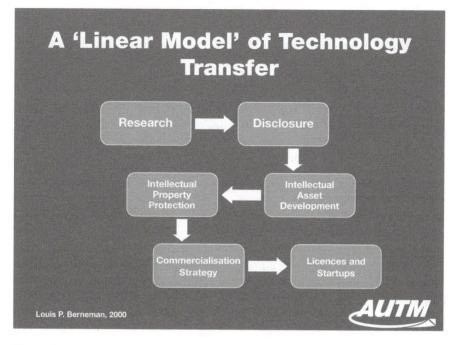

Figure 2

Source: © Louis P. Berneman, 2000. Used by permission.

a fraction of the total support needed by a university for its operation. TLO income will never be the primary source of funding for a university.

Figure 1, developed by Louis P. Berneman,[2] recent past President of AUTM, illustrates the relationship between industry and universities. Universities exist for the purposes of teaching, research and service. Universities value knowledge for the sake of knowledge, academic freedom and open discourse. On the other hand, industry values knowledge for its ability to impact the 'bottom line' and profitability. Industry prefers secrecy to protect trade secrets and the results of research from their competitors. But in the overlap between the university sector and industry sector, the TLOs exist. The TLOs are the interface between two different worlds; two different worlds that function very well independently. It is a challenge to successfully develop the relationships that work for collaboration between these two worlds.

In practice, TLOs have developed a 'linear model' of technology transfer (see Figure 2). Very seldom is research in a university performed specifically to develop an invention for the sole purpose of disclosure to a TLO. But, as researchers are now aware of the potential commercial value of the new ideas they create, they now have an opportunity to disclose those research results to a TLO. Then, the TLOs seek to manage those inventions on behalf of the faculty and the institution. The TLOs establish a project, and begin evaluating and managing that intellectual property. In the evaluation process, answers to many questions are sought: should we protect this property? Does its commercial value warrant protection? Then, we begin to develop a commercialisation strategy, seeking to find an industry partner, seeking to move the technology from the university to the commercial world. If successful, this linear process then culminates in the execution of a licence agreement with an industry partner willing to invest the resources necessary to bring a product to the market.

Historical perspective

At this juncture it would be useful to provide a historical perspective to the current practice. Prior to the Second World War, the scope of university research in the US was very limited; no more than twenty universities performed research of any significant amounts. US government funding of university research was insignificant. All changed, however, with the many technical requirements placed upon the government in the war effort. The government did not possess the internal resources to meet all its technology needs. So, it began to look to the universities, the non-profit sector, and to companies to develop many of its technical requirements.

At the conclusion of the Second World War, Dr Vannevar Bush, who was Chairman of the US Joint Research Development Board, prepared a report called 'Science, the Endless Frontier' and delivered it to President Franklin D. Roosevelt. In this report, he called for a large, on-going government investment in the development and application of science, to enhance the economy of the US by increasing the core pool of knowledge for use by industry. This report stimulated substantial and increasing government funding in research. The discussions led to the formation of the National Science Foundation, the National Institute of Health, and other government agencies focused upon the development of science and technology. It is often suggested that the concept of technology transfer was born in the report 'Science, the Endless Frontier'.

As the government first began working with the universities and non-profit sector, the question of intellectual property very seldom arose. But gradually, over time, as more and more contracts were initiated, the issue of ownership of IP began to occur. Furthermore, the government had never adopted a uniform patent policy. Thus, each federal agency funding research at universities began to develop its own intellectual property policies and rules. Thus, by the end of the 1960s, the universities accepting research funding from government agencies had more than 25 different intellectual property policies to negotiate.

Operating under these various government policies, the government had filed and held title to thousands of patents. Specifically, more than 28,000 government-owned patents had been filed; however, only 5 per cent of these patents were licensed to industry and even fewer of these inventions had resulted in any form of a commercial product. Therefore, the intended benefit of a patent policy to transfer technology into commercial products was not being realised with the practice of government ownership of the research results. A great debate took place regarding this dilemma in the 1970s. It was an emotional debate, arguing economic priorities versus academic priorities.

The debate in the late 1970s led to the passage of the Bayh-Dole Act in 1980 (P. L. 96–817). This Act was a fundamental change to the US patent law, a revolution, as it changed the ownership of the results of research funded by the US government. The Bayh-Dole Act established that title to inventions made with government funding at small businesses, universities and other non-profit entities belongs to those entities, and *not* to the government. A fundamental change occurred at this juncture. Congress examined the question, 'In whose hands, does the placement of the ownership of inventions serve the public's best interest?', which was posed by Howard Bremer. The Bayh-Dole Act intended to promote private investment in the commercialisation of industry-funded research in universities.

Howard Bremer, one of the participants in the debate in the 1970s and author of the publication, *University Technology Transfer: Evolution and Revolution*[3] has suggested that, prior to the Bayh-Dole Act, the government practice of ownership of the invention was inconsistent with the US patent law. The patent law in the US is designed to give to private citizens an incentive to promote the arts and science by protecting their rights in their original works of creativity or inventions. Yet, when the government owns the intellectual property rights, the patent is essentially a public property much like a publication.

Prior to the passage of the Bayh-Dole Act, private companies were very reluctant to invest their valuable resources necessary to make a commercial product from government-funded research results, as patents did not protect their investments. As Howard Bremer has stated, the US Congress determined that 'What is available to everyone is of interest to no one'. Furthermore, he notes that Bayh-Dole was a conclusion by the US Congress that (1) creativity is truly a national resource; (2) the patent system in the US is the vehicle which permits the delivery of the resource to the public; and (3) it is in the public interest to place stewardship of those research results in the creators in the hands of universities and small business. Congress recognised that existing US policy was simply ineffective at a time IP and innovation were becoming global currency. Bayh-Dole was a revolution, a fundamental change in the ownership of intellectual property rights resulting from university research.

Universities have certain obligations under the Bayh-Dole Act. It is beyond the scope of this chapter to mention all of them, but a few of the obligations might be noted. Under Bayh-Dole, universities must elect title to inventions they seek to commercialise. Once title is elected to an innovation, then the university must file a patent on elected inventions. Additionally, the Bayh-Dole Act gives preference to the licensing of inventions to small businesses; universities are encouraged to work with small businesses in their licensing efforts. Furthermore, in the case of an exclusive licence, the university's licensee must substantially manufacture the licensed product in the US, unless a waiver of that requirement is obtained from the US government. Additionally, the law specified how universities should manage income from licensing: universities must share a portion of the income with the inventor as an incentive to participate in the technology transfer process, and the balance must be used for research and educational purposes. And finally, the government retains the rights to use the intellectual property developed and patented by the university for governmental purposes only.

There were other forces at work in the 1980s. First, there was the Chakrabarty case (1980), wherein the US Supreme Court ruled that live-engineered microorganisms comprised patentable subject matter. This decision by the Supreme Court led to the genetic engineering and biotech industries that exploded in 1980s, in very close relationship with universities. Additionally, there was also enhanced national and international protection of patent rights recorded in the 1980s. In the US, the Federal Court System was reorganised for better enforcement of the infringement of patent rights. Finally, there was the emergence of the 'research university' in the 1970s and 1980s. With the end of the Cold War, government funding for research shifted from federal R&D to civilian R&D, particularly in health-related research. In this environment, the research university, with its research capabilities in biotechnology and medicine, has become even more important. As a consequence, there also grew a greater partnership between industry and academia in research in the 1980s, perhaps an unintended but positive consequence of the Bayh-Dole Act.

Results of this phenomenon have been unprecedented. First, the 'linear model' of technology transfer has been confirmed. It works! The linear process is a validated process now that complements the many other forms of technology transfer in institutions of higher education. With the passage of the Bayh-Dole Act, universities now have an incentive to protect their IP. Second, today more than 200 university TLOs have been established in North America. Third, as a consequence of Bayh-Dole, universities changed their own internal university policies to manage intellectual property rights in research relationships with non-governmental sponsors. Many states in the 1980s passed state laws regarding intellectual property management at state universities. For instance, Texas A&M University was required by the State of Texas in 1985 to put in place an intellectual property policy that copied the Bayh-Dole Act by requiring ownership of IP by the university rather than the State Government. Fourth, academic research is now critical to the nation's innovation and R&D capacity.

A recent study by the National Science Foundation indicated that 73 per cent of patents in the US today cite academic research in the patent application. Finally, as mentioned previously, there is strong incentive now for industry–university research collaborations.

The economic impact of these developments has been phenomenal. The Association of University Technology Managers (AUTM) conducts an annual survey of licensing activities in the US and Canada and has done so for the last nine years. The AUTM report for Fiscal Year 1999 demonstrated the significant economic impact of the technology transfer process in North America. In 1999, 344 new companies started from university research; since 1991, approximately 3,000 new companies have been created to commercialise the results of university research. In addition, consider the new products that meet unmet public needs; respondents to the AUTM survey reported that 470 new products entered the market place in 1999. AUTM estimates that more than 2,000 products are now on the market place based upon university technology transfer since the passage of the Bayh-Dole Act. The job creation impact also has been significant. The 1999 AUTM survey reported 270,900 jobs supported by product sales emerging from the license of university technologies. Finally, university technology transfer has resulted in a US$40.9 billion economic impact, with additional $5 billion in tax revenue.

An important conclusion can be made to this analysis of the economic impact: the benefits of the Bayh-Dole Act in the US were realised or accomplished without the US Congress appropriating any of the taxpayers' money for implementation of the Act. In the US, there are no national universities. Universities are a function of local, state, regional, or even municipal governments. So with the passage of the Bayh-Dole Act, these autonomous institutions were granted title to the intellectual property, and then were left to their own devices to develop the programmes and processes that transferred the research results to the public. The Bayh-Dole Act is a continuing 'national success story', representing the formation of a successful partnership between government, industry and academia.

With this foundation in the growth of the linear model of technology transfer through the TLOs, it is appropriate to focus a moment upon the growing role of the university in what is often called the new economy, the digital economy or even the knowledge economy. These words describe an economy that is becoming less dependent upon making and growing things, and more dependent upon the promotion of ideas and innovations. This new economy is less reliant upon natural resources and more dependent on human resources. In fact, perhaps the most significant need facing this new economy is the need for skilled technology workers. More than 300,000 information jobs were unfilled in 1998 with a prediction that the number will reach 2 million unfilled information jobs in the next ten years. *Red Herring* magazine recently identified its 'Top 10' critical issues for the Year 2001. It is interesting to note that the top three are 'computing, intellectual property, and venture capital'. It is no longer the 'first-world versus the third-world' in discussion of national economies; it is the competition of the 'fast-world versus the slow-world'.

The universities will have an even more important place or role in this new economy. First of all, the economic sectors with most rapid growth in the economy today are those closest to the science base, such as biotechnology, information resources, microelectronics, and new materials. These economic sectors are among the leading new business opportunities, as well as among the leading areas of research in academic institutions. Universities are idea factories. Ideas are like natural resources, and universities are a primary source of these ideas.

Universities will become more powerful as a source of innovation as industry needs more and more innovation to fuel business growth. It is my understanding that products today become obsolete at a pace more rapid than at any time in history. Thus, companies are searching for innovation and universities are sources of such innovation. Of course, the skilled knowledge workers will come from the universities. The Milken Institute has conducted a survey of the top 50 high-tech areas in the US and it found that, of the top 30 of those high-tech areas, 29 were home to a major research university. George Kozmetsky of IC[2] of the University of Texas, in a landmark study regarding the creation of the technopolis in 1988 stated that the nucleus for the new technopolis would be the university. The research university, he states:

> plays the key role in fostering research and development activities, the attraction of the key scholars and talented graduate students, the spinout of new companies, the attraction of major technology firms, a magnet for federal and private sector funding, and as a general source of ideas, employees and consultants for the high-tech industry.[4]

Zell Miller, who is a former governor of Georgia and now a professor at the University of Georgia, has stated: 'The future belongs to companies that can match innovation, and the ideas that drive technology forward with the educated workers who can make something literally out of those ideas. Both need the research and education that only universities can provide'.

This discussion obviously leads to the increasing role of universities and government in new business development in the new economy. It is only natural that as the economy becomes more entrepreneurial, and as high-tech companies focus upon biotechnology, advanced materials, microelectronics and other technologies important to university research initiatives, it becomes more and more important to our economies; universities also must participate in these diverse initiatives.

Additionally, in most instances, academic research discoveries are simply too early for established companies. This is the first challenge in a university technology licensing office: the challenge of transferring technologies that are too early in the product stage to interest established companies. Universities are not in the product development business; universities are in the business of research. Research takes an idea to a certain early stage of development, and then the universities are ready to transfer, handoff, or pass that idea to an industry partner for completion. Yet, from the industry perspective, the prospective licensee might say, 'Come back to see me when the product is finished.' Thus, there is a significant 'gap' in the product development stream. Start-up companies may fill this gap! Spin-off companies can step in, take the early stage technology, devote 'blood, sweat and tears' to development, and thereby reduce the risk.

Large companies, typically, are not focused upon taking forward the early stage technologies. Large companies, generally, are focused upon distribution and marketing of products today on a global scale. Once the spinout companies remove risks, larger companies may then be interested in acquisition to add value to their product portfolio. Spinout companies also contribute to the diversification of the university's research and service base. Additionally, support of university spinouts may meet carrier goals of many of the entrepreneurial faculty members who want to be involved in new companies. And last, creation of spinout companies gives universities the opportunity, as universities, to share in the upside in the value

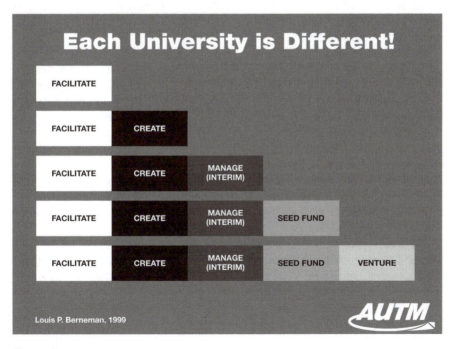

Figure 3

Source: © Louis P. Berneman, 1999. Used by permission.

creation of a new company. As licences are granted to spinouts, universities may take equity as consideration for the licence in lieu of other business considerations in the business arrangement. By doing so, universities can share in the value creation as that company grows and then either becomes a public company, or sells the equity in the company to a larger concern.

Louis P. Berneman, again, has created an excellent graph that shows that universities in the US today interface with spinout companies and entrepreneurial activities in many different ways (Figure 3). It is possible to find a different model for spinouts at every university in the US. Some universities simply facilitate the start-up of new companies. We introduce our new companies to business managers and venture capital firms. We can work with them to structure a licence agreement and can help them with cash flow problems in their initial stages of negotiation of the licence agreement. Yet, we do not get involved in creating the new company. As the graph shows, other universities can do much more in supporting start-up company creation, such as establishing incubators, and even assisting in the management to help spin them out. Finally, some universities are developing venture capital funds and seed funds to help new companies in their early stages. The seed funds might be a grant programme to help complete a prototype in early stage development of the product. Or, the funds may be an actual investment in the start-up companies. Many times, such investments are made by the university's endowment, development foundation or fund-raising organisation, rather than from actual university appropriation.

The question for a university as it considers participation in new business development in the US is this: will the university take a passive role or will it take an active role with the new spinout companies? In the US, there appears to be a distinct and noticeable difference between the capabilities of public universities and private universities in start-up company participation. Private universities are, perhaps, more innovative, more creative and more aggressive in interfacing with the spinout companies in new business creation than are the public universities. The laws of the state or the municipality limit many public universities. As a result, many public universities are creating non-profit corporations that are affiliated with the university that handle some of this interface with the new spinout companies.

There are rewards to the institution for its involvement in entrepreneurship and support of spinout companies. We have talked about some of these rewards, such as the new science and new technology that emerges with interface with the new companies; the employment opportunities for the graduate students; real-world experience for the graduate students and faculty, and so on. Participation in entrepreneurial activities enhances the institution's growth and its strength, especially in an economic and political environment where the state is looking to the university as 'the engine for economic development'. Participation in spinout creation contributes to the diversification of the research portfolio. For those faculty members who want to be involved in this process, such activities help us to retain the best and the brightest faculty members. Finally, such activities have the potential of creating great upside or great wealth for the institution as new companies become public or otherwise liquidate their assets.

But, not all is positive; such activities have the capability to impact the institution in a negative way. First, entrepreneurial activities may adversely impact the educational mission of the institution. The institution may become more market driven, more industry focused, which may lead to a shift away from scholarship to more of a consulting role to industry. Many conflicts of interest may arise in the management of the interests of scholarship versus the strong relationship to industry and spinout companies, both for the institution and individual faculty members.

Additionally, there are increased institutional and business costs incurred in the institution's involvement in start-up companies. Security laws are very complex and management of equity issues becomes complex which raises another area of specialty needed in the university; to understand how to take part in these initiatives to create new companies and own equity. Such activities may also create public relations challenges for the university. The headline for example, in the May 2000 issue of the *Atlantic Monthly* magazine was 'The Kept University: Corporations are providing more and more of the money for academic research, they want something in return and they are getting it'. The article also leads with this statement: 'Commercially sponsored research is putting at risk the paramount value of higher education – disinterested inquiry. Even more alarming, universities themselves are behaving more and more like for-profit companies.' The public relations challenges are real.

In summary, many universities in the US are struggling with the level and strength of their entry into the new knowledge-based economy: how entrepreneurial do they desire to be? How supportive will they be of spinout companies? There is no consensus from one university to another. As a generalisation, more and more universities are venturing into greater support of spinout companies and entrepreneurial activities in the academic environment.

The US government, also, is becoming more and more participatory, supporting entrepreneurship and encouraging innovation. In the US, the government does not fund TLOs, nor does the Federal Government directly fund universities. Rather, the government funds research and universities must compete for those research dollars. The US taxpayers desire the government to invest in people and workforce development. Addressing the shortage of skilled technical workers is a priority. Investing in infrastructure and in more research are also priorities. In the year 2000, the US government invested $71.2 billion in research activities. This number has been growing and will grow further, based upon Congressional and Presidential budget projections.

Second, the public expects the government to promote a conducive business climate for innovation, such as the removal of legal barriers to collaboration. In the State of Texas, for instance, the legislature is meeting and is working hard to remove several legal barriers in their ability to spin out companies in Texas's public universities. Finally, the US government should develop more entrepreneurial support programmes to enable private-sector investment in research and development, and in technology transfer. Changing the tax laws to give greater incentives to private industry to invest in university research could be an important example.

In conclusion, the twenty-first century will present a different economic setting. A new knowledge-based economy has supplanted the manufacturing economy that dominated the prior 100 years. The new economy uses intellectual capital rather than raw materials as its primary input. In addition, a new globalisation has emerged. Knowledge-based firms in the new economy are seeking educated and skilled workers. For all of these reasons and many others described in this chapter, universities will be the 'centrepiece' of this New World. Universities are the critical piece of the new innovation system; universities are uniquely in position to drive economic growth and social well being in the twenty-first century.

In our estimation, universities have made, and will continue to make, a significant and critical impact to the well being of our society, and the TLOs are, and will be, a critical component of this beneficial contribution. Ultimately, the success of a university TLO should not be measured by the number of licences, the amount of royalty income earned, the number of spinout firms or any of these traditional measures of performance. Rather TLOs should desire to maximise the value of their contributions to their customers, to the companies, the licensees of the innovations emerging from the institutions, and to maximise the value of the companies they help to create or spinouts. If TLOs are successful in maximising their value to their many clients and customers, they will then maximise their economic and social returns to the good of the public they serve.

Notes

1   This chapter contains the revised, updated text based on the plenary speech (hitherto unpublished) delivered at the International Technology Transfer Seminar in Tokyo, Japan in January 2001.
2   These graphs were created by Louis P. Berneman in the course of his lectures and research and are reproduced with his kind permission.
3   Howard Bremer (1998) *University Technology Transfer: Evolution and Revolution*, Washington, DC: Council on Government Relations (COGR), p. 18.
4   This quotation is from Raymond W. Smilor, David V. Gibson and George Kozmetsky (eds) (1988) *Creating the Technopolis: Linking Technology, Commercialization, and Economic Development*, Cambridge, MA: Ballinger, p. 150.
     Dr Kozmetsky was Director of the IC^2 Institute at the time of the publication. IC^2 Institute is an organisation administered by the University of Texas at Austin. The name represents Innovation, Creativity and Capital.

3 The role of entrepreneurship and venture businesses in redefining the value of intellectual property in Japan

Takuma Kiso

In order to envisage the role of entrepreneurship and venture businesses in redefining the value of intellectual property in Japan, it is very important to analyse the recent initiative of the Japanese government to make Japan a 'nation built on intellectual property'. In this chapter, after reviewing all the main points of the new initiative of the Koizumi administration, two aspects will be highlighted; how these efforts will encourage entrepreneurship and how they will promote the valuation of high-value added intangible assets. For the latter topic, the recent reports of METI and the Japan Patent Office (JPO) will be examined. Last, some of the remaining problems will be pointed out.

In his policy speech to the Diet in February 2002, Prime Minister Koizumi declared that he 'will set as one of our national goals that the results of research activities and creative endeavors are translated into intellectual properties that are strategically protected and utilised so that we can enhance the international competitiveness of Japanese industries'. Following this, the government created the *Strategic Council on Intellectual Properties*,[1] and made the *Intellectual Property Policy Outline* in July of the same year. In March 2003, the *Basic Law on Intellectual Property* came into effect and the *Intellectual Property Policy Headquarters* was established, and in July 2003 the *Programme for Promoting the Creation, Protection, and Exploitation of Intellectual Properties* was released.

The *Programme for Promoting the Creation, Protection, and Exploitation of Intellectual Properties*

In this section, the programme, which lays out some 270 measures, will be reviewed. It consists of five chapters. The first three chapters deal with various steps to create, protect, and utilise intellectual properties, respectively. The fourth chapter specifically discusses ideas for the dramatic expansion of the media content business, and the last chapter suggests ways to develop human resources related to intellectual property and to improve public awareness of intellectual property. Many of these 270-odd steps will be concluded in one way or another within FY2003 and the remaining ones will be resolved by the end of FY2004. Each measure has been clearly assigned to a ministry or ministries.

The first chapter deals with creation of intellectual properties. Within the recognition that the production of creative and innovative research and development results is the basis of a 'nation built on intellectual property', the administration has made it very clear that the main role of universities and public research organisations is to make contributions to the society in the form of creation of intellectual property. Universities and public research institutes with many R&D resources are encouraged to create excellent intellectual properties including inventions, software, and databases by various measures suggested. In order to clarify this policy, the government will allocate its funds and other resources on the basis of general intellectual property indicators which reflect the number of filed patents, the number and revenue of licensing, the number of quoted patents, records of joint research projects and of starting businesses, and the number of consultations in addition to the traditional number and quality of research papers. This means that the government will change its criteria for allocation of R&D budgets to universities and public research institutes. The administration, at the same time, emphasises the quality rather than the quantity of intellectual properties, directing universities and public research institutes to pursue basic patents.

It is also suggested that Article 35 of Japan's Patent Law should be abolished or revised in FY2004. It stipulates how corporate employees should be rewarded for their inventions but does not really apply to the current situation in which an increasing number of corporate researchers have now filed lawsuits against their employers for appropriate compensation for the former's inventions.

The second chapter argues for stronger protection of intellectual properties from two viewpoints.

The first part of this chapter begins by stating that proper protection of intellectual properties is indispensable in order to reinforce incentives for creation of intellectual properties, and to effectively exploit them. In order to reduce a backlog of 500,000 pending applications and to cope with an expected 300,000 new applications, for example, the *Law to Ensure Prompt Examination of Patent Applications* (tentative title) will be presented to the ordinary Diet session of FY2004. According to *Yomiuri Shimbun* (27 August 2003), at the moment applicants in Japan wait for 2 years on average for their examinations to actually start after their applications. This waiting period is longer than those seen in the US and Europe (16.7 months and 20.7 months, respectively). Therefore, the Patent Office plans to hire fixed-term examiners. The same daily reports that the Patent Office intends to increase the number of examiners by 500 from the present 1,100. The term of office of the examiners will be limited to 10 years and 100 examiners will be hired each year over the coming 5 years.

Establishment of an Intellectual Property High Court is another feature in this part. This is for enhancement of a dispute settlement system and the related laws will be presented to the ordinary Diet session of FY2004. It has been highly praised that the recent revision of the Code of Civil Procedure has already given the Tokyo High Court a jurisdiction over lawsuits related to intellectual properties. But the creation of a new High Court, which handles cases related only to IP, will clearly show to the world that Japan is aiming at becoming a nation built on intellectual property.

The second section of the protection chapter takes up safeguards against counterfeits and pirated copies. The reason for this section is a well-known fact among the Japanese people and enterprises: that knockoffs, or fake brand-name products, are prevalent in China and other Asian countries, infringing on trademarks. Now reports about infringements on design rights and patents are on the increase and unauthorised copies of such digital contents as music and animations from Japan are mass-marketed in the region. The programme quotes the Copyright Research and Information Center (CRIC) in Japan as saying that damage caused by China's infringement on 'contents', or copyrighted works, amounts to 2 trillion yen per year and Union De Fabrican in France as saying that damage brought about by infringement of trademark such as brand-name products amounts to 500 billion yen per year. The JPO started to release the *Report on Damages Caused by Counterfeit Goods* (tentative translation) last year. The FY2002 edition points out that, regardless of industries and types of intellectual property, the largest damages can be found in the Asia region, especially in China, Taiwan and Korea. So the JPO did an individual survey in these three countries and Thailand and proposed the strengthening of measures to interdict smuggling at the border.

The third chapter focuses on the exploitation of IP. Even if more intellectual properties are created faster and protected more properly, if they are left unutilised they will become a waste of treasure. Utilisation of trust or a fiduciary system for management of patents and for the liquidation of patents is one of the main points of this chapter. The Council for Financial Services proposed, in July 2003, that subjects of trust businesses should be deregulated and could include intellectual properties. Accordingly, the Trust Business Law will be modified next year.

Another item worth mentioning is stronger protection of licensees in the case of licensers going bankrupt.

The fourth chapter is significant for global competition. The government declares that, under the recognition that Japan's digital contents industries such as movies, animation and video games have a comparative advantage globally, it has set dramatic development of these industries as vital. Activities of creators of digital contents will be more easily funded by easing the related regulations and rules and by introducing a credit guarantee system. The government also plans to support the marketing of digital contents into foreign countries.

The programme is concluded by the fifth chapter entitled 'Development of human resources and raising awareness of the Japanese people of the value of intellectual properties'. In order for Japan to make a nation built on IP, those who need to be encouraged are not only those who create intellectual properties but also specialists who protect them as patent rights, settle the related disputes, and make licensing agreements. In this context, the first priority will be given to an increase in the number of lawyers specialising in intellectual properties and of patent attorneys who show tough international competitiveness. This objective will be achieved by the establishment of such professional schools as law schools and business schools with a Management of Technology (MOT) programme.

In the following sections, some of the specific suggestions are pointed out in the context of: (1) encouragement of entrepreneurship among universities, public research institutes, and individuals; and (2) valuation of intellectual properties.

Encouragement of entrepreneurship

In the overview, the programme clearly states that one of the things in need of special attention for Japan to become a nation built on intellectual properties is to support small- and medium-sized enterprises and venture businesses.

Some of the items in the programme are, therefore, to ease transfer of intellectual properties, potential seeds of new and future businesses, from universities and public research institutes to the private sector.

More specifically, the programme requests universities and public research institutes, reservoirs of IP, to play a central role in the encouragement of entrepreneurship. These entities will be told to make and enhance a system of returning their intellectual properties to the society through much more active TLOs and college-launched venture businesses.

Their staff members, who are the main creators of intellectual properties, will also be motivated. When a college/a public research institute takes over rights of invention of its staff members and obtains licence fees, then the staff members will be entitled to a part of them. New rules of the reward payment will be laid down.

Flexible rules will be developed for the transfer of rights and registration of licences, and applied to a researcher who thinks of setting up a new business by utilising his/her research results obtained at colleges/public research institutes. The government hopes that this measure will promote college-launched venture businesses.

Abolition or revision of the rewards of company employees for their inventions stipulated in the Japanese Patent Law, which was touched upon earlier, is also expected to stimulate entrepreneurship.

The Japanese Bayh-Dole Act will be enforced fully so that intellectual properties obtained through the execution of research commissioned by the

Japanese government and special public corporations may belong to commissioned researchers. The government also will concentrate on informing SMEs so that they will realise the importance of having their innovative techniques patented and exploiting them.

Valuation of intellectual properties

For the purposes of valuation of intellectual properties, an establishment of proper methods is one of the main issues in the third chapter. The programme says that what should be rules to objectively valuate intellectual properties will be discussed and organised by FY2004 on the basis of methods developed by various private research organisations. In addition, the government will try to establish a market for intellectual properties by gathering and disclosing actual valuations of intellectual properties in the case of M&As which are expected to boom.

Concurrently, measures to appropriately evaluate patents are also being introduced. In order to enhance the understanding of financial markets about IP, the feasible guideline of disclosure on intellectual property has been started in FY2003. Regulations concerning the manner of recording and disclosing of intellectual property on financial statements began discussions in FY2003.

In order to elaborate what has been discussed in Japan, reports by METI and the JPO are worth looking at.

In June 2002, METI released a report entitled *Report of the Study Group on Brand Evaluation.*[2]

In March 2003, the JPO published a report entitled 'Study on Patent Valuation System in Patent Trading Markets'[3] in which it commissioned the Japan Institute of Invention and Innovation. This report extensively discusses patent valuation.

In the first chapter, the JPO report summarises the significance and role of the patent valuation system in patent trading markets as follows: (1) patent valuation systems play a role of supporting tool for top executives who run enterprises on the basis of intellectual property as managerial resources; (2) the system will be positioned as the axis of restructuring on the basis of a new process of value formation; (3) standardisation of patent valuation methods is expected to strengthen the environment for competitive markets; (4) through the patent valuation system, small- and medium-sized enterprises as well as large firms reassess their potential growth; (5) the patent valuation scheme is an essential tool for the trade of patents, promotion of patent transfer, and the securitisation of patents.

In the second chapter, the report shows survey results on utilisation of various types of patent valuation system. In order to grasp the needs and problems of private enterprises, universities, and TLOs related to patent valuation systems, a questionnaire was sent to 2,500 entities including companies listed on the first and second sections of the Tokyo Stock

Exchange and unlisted companies with 500 or more employees. Six hundred and ninety-five, or 27.8 per cent of the recipients, answered it. Some of the most salient points are as follows:

1 Patents are regarded important from the viewpoint of business strategy, but are not fully exploited.
2 Many of the respondents look for establishment of schemes to objectively estimate patent value and to promote patent trading.
3 A little less than a half of respondents evaluate their patents now. Monetary value is emphasised when technology transfer is considered while relative (non-monetary) assessment is focused in the case of patent application. And patent valuation has become more important within a company as an asset and/or for calculation of rewards for employees' invention.
4 Specialists, know-how and knowledge of patent valuation are insufficient at respondent companies.
5 Respondents find it difficult to economically evaluate patents.
6 Respondents hope to make public such pieces of information as business practices of licensing and standard royalty rate in each industry.
7 Patent Valuation Indicator (Value Assessment Indicator)[4] of the JPO is utilised by only 6 per cent of the respondents while it is known by more than 50 per cent of them.
8 About 50 per cent of the respondents want a guideline for patent evaluation, information on patent evaluation methods currently available, or opening and building a database necessary for patent evaluation.

The third chapter compares and analyses various types of patent valuation systems. In its first section, the report briefly introduces three main methods with their merits and demerits respectively. In an income approach (an absolute value estimation), patent value is determined by the summation of a stream of future economic contribution (or income). The point is whether or not the contribution of intellectual property can be appropriately separated from the total cash flow of an enterprise or its products. In a market approach (a relative value estimation), patent value is estimated by transaction prices of the similar intellectual properties. In reality, however, intellectual properties are rarely traded independently in markets, making this method not practically applicable. In a cost approach (a replacement cost estimation), patent value is calculated as the costs of remaking the intellectual property dealt with at this moment. This approach is applicable to the patents which can be duplicated only if their development costs are covered. In the real world, however, the same amount of development and research costs does not necessarily lead to the same invention. Or the exploitation of the patents may bring more economic value than the developments cost. Therefore, the third approach is insufficient for the patents' economic valuation.

In the second section of the third chapter of the JPO report, two viewpoints are discussed for the patent valuation. The first aspect is the purpose of valuation. The report picks five major purposes: (1) posting the patent value in financial statements; (2) deciding royalty rates; (3) trade of patents; (4) evaluation of technology development-oriented venture businesses for their capital increase or public offering; and (5) securitisation of patents. Each purpose requires a different approach of patent valuation. The second viewpoint is what is to be patented. Individual patents and a group of patents (or a patent portfolio) need different methods of valuation. Patents to be traded and those to be strategically positioned within a company require different methods of valuation. Patents already applied to products (or commercialised), those to be applied to products, and those not to be applied to products come under different valuation procedures. Non-utilised patents tend to be undervalued, because their owners do not know how to exploit them, requiring appropriate evaluation methods for promoting their trades. The third section of this chapter thoroughly explains the various methods of valuation.

For the relative value estimation of patents, three methods are presented. The Patent Valuation Indicator (in case of technology transfer) was devised and released by the JPO in 1999. The indicator will be calculated on the basis of three factors: characteristics of the patent (technological dominance and completeness), transferability (reliability of technology transfer and stability of the patent), and commercial potential (commercialisation possibility and profitability). The valuation system of Nihon IR[5] is based on the Patent Valuation Indicator of the JPO but is more objective by clarifying the purpose of patent valuation. The Nomura Research Institute's Patent Portfolio Management (NRIPPM) is a tool used for searching valid patents effectively.

For the monetary value estimation of patents, three methods of income approaches, market approaches and cost approaches, are elaborated. For the income approaches, DCF (discount cash flow) methods, real option methods and relief from royalty methods are discussed. For the market approaches, sales comparison approaches and the TRRU[6] valuation system devised by PL-X[7] are introduced. And for the cost approach, replacement cost methods and historic costs approaches are discussed. This chapter does not intend to be too technical about each of these methods.[8]

The fourth section of the report points out that the number of companies providing patent valuation services started to increase from around 2000. The report says that, although the potential for patent evaluation may be large, there exist only a few specialist companies in Japan. The report, in fact, introduces the following companies; Yet2.com, PL-X, Nihon IR and QED Intellectual Property.[9]

The fourth chapter discusses measures to diffuse and spread patent valuation systems. The first measure, as is often the case, is the development of human resources. Staff are required who not only evaluate patents but also those who can exploit patents in actual businesses and build appropriate systems. Second, the paper emphasises the needs of data collection for patent evaluation, suggesting seven measures. (1) Devising simple computer software for calculation of business valuation with the least amount of data. For this purpose, (2) making a web site for intellectual property evaluation so that people and companies concerned can have access to the relevant data including the related statistics. (3) Making a database of statistics on management indicators which can be sorted by industries, technologies, and company sizes. (4) Setting various parameters derived from the statistical data. (5) Collecting and making available such information on licensing as royalty rates and their determinants in order to see the realities of transactions of intellectual properties. (6) Making and continuing to show useful parameters by statistically analysing survey results on the realities of transactions of intellectual properties. (7) Analysing the effects of intellectual properties by industries and the size of corporations by use of macro-economic indicators and reinforcing valuation of individual intellectual properties.

Third, the chapter deals with accounting problems of intellectual property. The chapter picks three of the most controversial issues. The first matter is capitalising costs of research and development as intangible assets. In the US and Japan, research and development are basically expenses and the total costs of development are annotated. The point is whether the costs of successful researches and failed ones should be separated or not. The second topic is deciding valuation of intellectual property. When a company purchases an intellectual property, there will be no problem recording the value of this asset as its price. If, however, a company merges with another one, and the laws and regulations require the intellectual properties to be evaluated, the methods of evaluation are at issue. The third problem is disclosing additional information pertinent to IP especially when the costs of research and development cannot be posted on the balance sheets. These issues are further elaborated by referring to SFAS[10] #2 (Accounting for Research and Development Costs),[11] #141 (Business Combinations)[12] and #142 (Goodwill and Other Intangible Assets)[13] issued by FASB[14] of the US; IAS 38 (Intangible Assets)[15] of IAS,[16] and FRS[17] #7 (Fair Values in Acquisition Accounting)[18] of UK; and Business Accounting Principles[19] for Balance Sheets 5-E (Intangible Assets)[20] of Japan.

The section is concluded by predicting that companies willing to meet the strong request of investors to disclose information related to intellectual property will gradually and voluntarily disclose numerical data of IP using their own measurement standards.

For the disclosure of information on patents and technology, METI released a pilot model in March 2003.

The fifth and last chapter of the report suggests the outline of patent valuation systems in the context of promotion of patent trading. The first and most urgent factor is making and publicising cases of intellectual property valuation. Many more cases of patent trade should be disclosed, such as those in the real estate industry. The points to be disclosed may include assessment of patent transfer value, royalties for licensing, weight of technology (patents) to business income by industry. The second pillar is making a simple valuation system of intellectual property. Here, the word 'simple' has several aspects. One is that the valuation method should be objective, highly reliable, and quick so that companies can easily and safely decide the transfer of their patent and licensing. Another point is that different methods, for example, absolute/relative value estimation and simple/highly accurate estimation, should be provided so that the owners of patents can utilise one of them, depending on their needs. The third element is making an appropriate subsidy system and a patent valuation agency. A subsidy is needed in order to cover the costs of initial investment of companies to develop a patent valuation system including personnel training. Technological assessment of patents can be done by enterprises themselves, while legal assessments can be made by patent attorneys. But economic assessment is very difficult especially if it should be objective. So the establishment of a patent valuation agency which comprehensively and quickly evaluates all the three aspects is expected to vitalise the patent distribution market. A new qualification may be necessary. Someone like a 'trader of intellectual property'[21] should be introduced. Like lawyers and certified public accountants, the traders can utilise their past experiences of patent transfer while they keep the cases secret. In addition to these, the report proposes a combined use of lump sum payment for licensing, which reflects on development costs of patents, and running royalty, which is based on profit distribution, and creation of a community for patent transfer which is a network of people specialising in, and interested in, patent valuation.

Remaining challenges

Returning to the *Programme for Promoting the Creation, Protection, and Exploitation of Intellectual Properties*, this section will assess the programme and some of the remaining challenges will be discussed here.

The programme is basically very well accepted. A statement by the National Forum for Intellectual Property Strategy is worth noting. The forum is a non-profit group of intellectual property specialists and headed by one of the former commissioners of the JPO. It has been leading the discussion of IP in Japan, and has scrutinised the programme. Therefore it would be a good idea to introduce their arguments here, together with other comments found in newspapers.

The forum gives especially high marks to the following points:

In the second chapter (protection of intellectual property)

- Making of the *Law to Ensure Prompt Examination of Patent Applications.*[22]
- Development and utilisation of organisations of prior-art search: measures will be taken in and after FY2004 to expand and improve the functions of prior-art search organisations in the private sector so that universities and corporations can properly determine the patentability of their research results before they file an application for examination. Also promoted are the publication of search tools for prior art and the transfer of know-how of prior-art search, both held by the JPO. From the viewpoint of higher efficiency and more prompt and adequate examination, it is expected that conclusions will be drawn by the end of FY2003/early FY2004 on conditions for newly designated search organisations, a system for prior-art searches done by designated search organisations at the request of applicants, and the pros and cons of requiring applicants to do prior-art searches.
- Reinforced protection of trade secrets: the programme states that the guideline of unintended leakage of metal mould design and metal mould manufacturing data (released in July 2002) and the guideline of trade secret management (released in January 2003) will be publicised as much as possible. It also suggests that strengthened protection of test data of drugs and medicines will be explored by the end of FY2005.
- Establishment of an Intellectual Property High Court.[23]

In the third chapter (exploitation of intellectual property)

- Strategic strengthening of international standardisation activities: for research and development activities whose results will have a potential to be spread widely and to influence the society in the future, the government encourages and assists people and institutes concerned to make a strategic vision for standardisation in Japan. At the same time the government encourages them to participate in international standardisation activities. In short, the government is directing researchers towards making the results of their research and development into a 'global standard'.
- Reinforcement of the stability of intellectual property licence contracts in the case that a licensor has gone bankrupt.

In the fourth chapter (media content business)

- Simplification of Japan's Copyright Act.

The forum, at the same time, has regarded the following points as a basis for further discussion.

In the second chapter of the protection of intellectual property, the forum opposes proposed acceleration and delay of examinations depending on the applicants' needs. The reason behind this is that some of the measures are in favour of big businesses. The group, at the same time, is critical of the fact that measures against counterfeits and pirated copies are only half-finished. The draft programme included an establishment of a quasi-judicial organisation similar to the United States International Trade Commission which is empowered to promptly block illegal imports. This agenda, however, was opposed by the Ministry of Finance which has control of the Customs House. It is said that the Ministry does not like the idea of an organisation equivalent to the US International Trade Commission over-riding the Customs House. On the other hand, *Nihon-Keizai Shimbun*, or Japan's Financial Times, accused the Supreme Court of objecting to the participation of engineers in patent-related trials[24] while the court considers introducing a system of the participation of ordinary people into serious criminal cases, something similar to the jury system in the US.

The National Forum for Intellectual Property Strategy requests the government to further discuss ways of better communication of the Patent Office with applicants and the means of stronger protection of patents related to medical practice, designs, and trademarks.

In the fifth chapter on the development of human resources and aware-ness-raising of the general public on IP, the programme states that the government will discuss whether or not the Intellectual Property Law should be included in elective subjects of Japan's bar examination. But the forum strongly proposes that this inclusion should be decided within 2003. Other-wise, plans to create intellectual property law schools will not proceed, delaying enforcement of intellectual property through well-trained experts.

Concluding remarks

In this chapter, the current situation and future direction of systems surrounding Japan's intellectual property has been described.

Although there continues to be some remaining tasks, Japan is now firmly moving towards an intellectual property-oriented country, especially from the side of the judicial branch of the government. In fact, Prof. Katsuya Tamai of the University of Tokyo once said that the highest-calibre judges are now sent to the section related to intellectual property and their court decisions are translated into English immediately and dispatched around the world.

Although Japan's start in the current intellectual property race was 20 years delayed in terms of the systematic circle of creation, protection and exploitation, the country will soon catch up with the other industrialised countries and is already moving ahead rapidly in the area of valuation.

Together with manufacturers with many inventions patented and producers of Pokemon animation, computer games, and movies like *Zatoichi* whose director won 'best director' at the sixtieth Venice Film Festival, Japan will surely succeed in making a nation built on intellectual property once more.

Notes

1 Italics show tentative translations by the Japanese government. *Strategic Council on Intellectual Properties* is an organisation that was established as an advisory committee to the Prime Minister in March 2002. Its creation was decided one month earlier in February 2002. *Intellectual Property Policy Outline* is the name of an outline of a policy package made and released by the Council (No. 1) in July 2002. *Basic Law on Intellectual Property* is the name of a new law made in December 2002 and implemented in March 2003. This measure is included in Policy Outline (No. 2). *Intellectual Property Policy Headquarters* is a standing governmental office established at the Cabinet which promotes IP policies. This measure is included in Policy Outline (No. 2). *Programme for Promoting the Creation, Protection, and Exploitation of Intellectual Properties* is a policy package with details that was made and released by the Headquarters in July 2003. This measure is included in Policy Outline (No. 2). *Law to Ensure Prompt Examination of Patent Applications* is the name of a new law. This measure is included in Programme (No. 5).
2 The original Japanese title is '*Burando Kachi-hyouka Kenkyu-kai Houkoku-sho*'. Akito Tani explains this report thoroughly in Chapter 8.
3 The original Japanese title is '*Tokkyo-Ryutsu-Shijo ni okeru Tokkyo-Kachi-Hyouka Shisutemu ni kannsuru Chousa*'.
4 The original Japanese is '*Tokkyo-Hyouka-Shihyou (Kachi-Hyouka-Shihyou)*'.
5 Nihon IR is a company specialising in patent-related information. Its homepage does not tell the origin of the company name but Nihon means Japan and IR probably stands for information retrieval.
6 TRRU stands for Technology Risk/Reward Unit.
7 PL-X stands for Patent and Licence Exchange.
8 Explanation of these accounting methods has been covered by Ruth Taplin in the introductory chapter of this book.
9 For further explanation of QED policies, please see Quentin Vailes's chapter, 'Intellectual Property Licensing – A History of Japan's Continuing Corporate Advantage' in *Exploiting Patent Rights and a New Climate for Innovation in Japan*, ed. Ruth Taplin 2003 by IPI.
10 Statement of Financial Accounting Standards.
11 Please see the following site: http://www.fasb.org/pdf/fas2.pdf
12 Please see the following site: http://www.fasb.org/pdf/fas141.pdf
13 Please see the following site: http://www.fasb.org/pdf/fas142.pdf
14 Financial Accounting Standards Board.
15 Please see the following site: http://www.iasc.org.uk/cmt/0001.asp?n=982&s=10095039&sc={F016DBE7-BE95-4C13-B80F-C49238AAC2E1}&sd=761139202
16 International Accounting Standards.
17 Financial Records Systems.
18 Please see the following site: http://www.asb.org.uk/publications/publication138.html
19 The original Japanese is '*Kigyo-Kaikei Gensoku*'.
20 Please see the following site, for example, for the original Japanese text: http://kai-kei.ceo-jp.com/ks/kg.htm

21 The original Japanese is '*Chiteki-Zaisan Torihiki Ryutsu-Shi*'.
22 See p. 34 (this chapter) for the details.
23 Ibid.
24 According to *Nihon Keizai Shimbun* (27 October 2003), the government suggests that engineers without a lawyer's qualification should be included in the new Intellectual Property High Court although it should be discussed further if they are treated as judges or assistants to judges.

References

Cabinet, *Programme for Promoting the Creation, Protection, and Exploitation of Intellectual Properties*, July 2003.

Ministry of Economy, Trade and Industry, *Report of the Study Group on Brand Evaluation*, June 2002.

Ministry of Economy, Trade and Industry, *A Pilot Model for Disclosure of Information on Patents and Technology*, March 2003.

National Forum for Intellectual Property Strategy, *Opinions about the Programme for Promoting the Creation, Protection, and Exploitation of Intellectual Properties (draft)*, June 2003.

Patent Office, *Study on Patent Valuation System in Patent Trading Market*, March 2003.

4 Understanding how IP is valued in Japan in relation to medicine

Tomoyuki Hisa[1]

The valuation of intellectual property is, in general, standardised by the valuation of monetary issues. However, it is an evaluation at the societal level that counts when it comes to medical issues. Although this attitude seems native to Japan, it would appear that such a socially important issue as medicine is an exception from intellectual property from the point of view of it existing to serve the public. Similarly, university academism may also be considered to be an exception due to its socially prominent nature and traditional distance from commercialisation.

History with regard to Japan

Such attitudes have emanated from the engineering departments of universities that represent a traditional way of thinking about intellectual property in Japanese society. During the period Meiji Ishin (Restoration during the Meiji Era) that occurred in the eighteenth century, Japan embarked on a course of modernisation. At that time, there were no universities in Japan as we know them today. Instead, first of all, personnel training centres were created where people were given an education about technology so as to further Japan in promoting industrial business. Subsequently, people who obtained scientific knowledge and skills through training (although they were few in number) took up jobs to both teach at a training centre and to manage industrial business in a senior capacity.

In 1886, however, the Engineering Department of Tokyo University came under the jurisdiction of the Ministry of Education. An attitude began to spread that expressed the idea that research and education involving private and main enterprises was not academic and a trend was instituted that university researchers must not retain intellectual property rights. In addition, this trend of denying university researchers having intellectual property rights gained increasing public support. This is because, throughout the Sino-Japanese War, Russo-Japanese War, the First World War and the Second World War, military sectors were combined with industrial sectors and university researchers who were forced to cooperate with the Army began to deny the existence of such military–industrial complexes to survive.

In 1973, the Ministry of Education issued a memorandum to state universities. The memorandum contained the more advantageous condition for researchers that invention, in principle, belongs to the researcher. Exceptions were: (1) when a researcher used a large-scale device; (2) when a researcher received a grant for the purpose of invention; (3) when there is a special regulation in law; and (4) when a researcher hands over his rights to the state. Despite this fact, however, an overall trend continued that researchers were not entitled to intellectual property rights.

However, following the collapse of the Berlin Wall in the early 1990s when the conflict between East–West ideologies ceased, both industrial sectors and universities began joint research and development. In the engineering departments, ideas concerning IPR began to gain acceptance.

In 1998, the TLOs were established and a market on which to trade the fruits of research was established. In 2004, it became a state university corporation and this phenomenon is said to be a Japanese version of the era of Bayh-Dole.[2]

Contrary to this, in the case of medical study, medicine and doctors all enjoy a high status and reputation in Japanese society and it has been considered as inappropriate to value a doctor's skills through the simple calculation of amounts of money. There was a saying that all other payments were settled by cash but rewards for doctors and artists were settled by old money.

The role of a doctor was seen to be a humanitarian one, being especially scientific at a high level as well as being independent from politics and administration. Doctors were considered to be professionally independent and, from the point of view of a humanitarian stance, there were many who stood against certain government policies such as a demand for cooperation in war. In addition, there were MPs who originally were doctors or who were recommended by the association of doctors.

As a result of this, there was no acceleration in change of attitude in the medical sector compared with that of the engineering sector; especially, since there was an emphasis on the public nature of such socially important issues such as medicine. Therefore, the government upheld a policy that it redistributed taxes collected from companies to medical researchers so that it could retain a rule, in principle, that companies and medical researchers should be prevented from having a common interest in a direct relationship. However, there were a few cases in which companies and medical researchers were connected directly by using the method of long-term multiple settlement.

In other words, medical researchers have been engaged solely in research. Although they have no interest in transforming their achievements into intellectual property, they required research funding. Of course, they would not know how to apply for a patent concerning the results of their research, and if this would then lead to business enterprise. This would necessitate money spent on the patent application and for commercialisation. Medical researchers do not have enough funds to afford these.

Therefore, companies donate a few million yen annually to 100–200 research units that are under the auspices of famous medical researchers working at well-known universities. While university medical researchers can conduct research work by utilising such funds and making contributions to the inventions by producing and publishing a thesis about such innovations, it is companies whose donated funds pay for the resulting patents. However, a few problems arose with this method.

1   It was ineffective.

    a   An intellectual property that has low potential at the market level is given to a company.

    b   Although the resulting innovation may be a useful intellectual property, it does not necessarily lie within a company's specialised field and as intellectual property would then be left unused.

2   This kind of relationship is based on the long term and a relationship of trust.

    a   No transparency exists. That means there is no clear distinction between research donations and any rebate. (However, two regulations were instituted – Occupation Moral Regulation in 1996 and a Governmental Officer Moral Regulation in 2000 – to deal with this matter and the situation has improved in recent times to a certain extent.)

    b   It would take on a closed relationship like a Guild since there would not be an opportunity for a new company or new researcher to enter. (However, it is beyond the scope of this chapter to concentrate only on the negative and problematic side of this point.) This guild-like organisation has positive aspects as it supports long-term research, rather than short-term and it prevents research falling into the hands of American-style strategic venture capital.

    c   This scale of funding does not reach small- and medium-size enterprises which would cause difficulties in establishing a smaller-scale venture.

Government intervention

In tandem, the government launched a strategy to diminish the independence of doctors from politics and administration and promoted this strategy methodically. In other words, it was a strategy by which the government both increased the number of low-level doctors and lowered the social status of high-level doctors. In addition, the government made low-level doctors compete with their other established colleagues on the marketplace so that doctors were losing their financial power as well.

During the Second World War, a special medical institute was established where students studied for a shorter period and could obtain a medical qualification without attending and graduating from university. This institute was mainly used to train army doctors. In addition, after war time, there was a policy that meant every one of the prefectures had at least one medical university. However, in practice such an educational institute was a semi-university designed only for medical study and taught at a low standard and it did not become a formal university for political reasons. Recently, after it was confirmed that this strategy worked successfully and the independence of doctors became diminished, the government has been trying to systematise and integrate these medical universities into centres of higher learning because it could reduce both the governmental expenditure and the number of governmental officials.

IP gains in status

In the university sectors in general and in the engineering departments in particular, as mentioned above, there has been a shift in perceptions about the acquisition of IPR from being a bad to being a good thing. When the recruitment process takes place for professors and research workers, a particularly marked change may be noted. In addition to publications, theses and presentations at academic conferences, an evaluation standard began to include finding out about the existence or non-existence of a patent in relation to the applicants' inventions, which became eventually a positive evaluation of the invention.

Beforehand, there was a tendency for a researcher to hide the fact that a patent had been obtained as though it had been gained due to a fear that questions may arise about being dishonourable about money. Alternatively, researchers feared that they might be seen to have an unsound close relationship with companies and this would result in their work being evaluated in a negative light. In medical departments of universities, a majority of clinical trial doctors exist who view patenting negatively. However, there is a tendency among researchers of basic medical studies to be willing to obtain a patent both because their post is a serious issue in their career and because a patent is expected to bring a positive outcome in any evaluation.

When asked, ordinary Japanese people reflect the idea that medical studies and medicine are becoming less special or that the mystique is waning. For example, people are demanding first of all an introduction of the principle of competition into all sectors of medical studies and medicine. They are also demanding an improvement in deficit-suffering public hospitals into ones with surpluses through efficient management and a restriction on the total national health expenditure that is designed for

Japanese citizens since the government claims that it is reducing the expenditure (but in my opinion is not being candid with the public).

However, when the Japanese people are asked a question that deals with much deeper issues, they believe that doctors will give patients medical treatment that is both of high quality and inexpensive. They also want a guarantee of free access to treatment coupled with care being given as if the doctor is treating his own family member. It seems that they have failed in understanding that they cannot obtain such service if a strictly business-based model is to be followed. In other words, they will have to wait in the queue if the treatment given is of both high quality and cheap, and treatment will be necessarily expensive if it is of both high quality and with free, rapid access. In addition, it is natural to think that if a treatment is cheap and given freely, it becomes low quality. If the government reduces the total national health expenditure, it is clear that medical resources people expect to receive will diminish in amount and quality. People are speaking and raising their voices, without fully understanding the fact that it is impossible to ask hospital management teams that have introduced a principle of competition for family-like treatment. It seems as if the Japanese population have not understood that they have been asking for a policy at the opposite end of the medical goal they have been pursuing.

From the cases we reviewed, the social reputation concerning the valuation of intellectual property in the Japanese medical sectors has changed. It is assumed, according to the results, that it may be a possibility that the medical sector can no longer be an exception in the future.

Why did a change in the perception by Japanese society about intellectual property occur? It has not followed cases of the US and changes in Europe. America advocates pro-patenting aggressively, claiming that it is a global standard, and then resorts to a strategy to cash in on patent charges; Japan has to fight back in my estimation. Otherwise, Japan will be asked to settle a huge payment for a patent and helplessly let America take all the profits despite the fact that research and production derives from Japan. In addition, Japan cannot compete with the cheap labour force in China in terms of production. From this basis, Japan is now shifting from an economic society in which mass production and mass consumption is an ultimate proposition, to an economic society that is based on the creation and distribution of information. This new high-level information society can only survive by establishing a new social system that realises a free act of creation, distribution and sharing of information and knowledge that is the property which human beings intellectually created and that harmonises life/division, industry/economy and nature/environment as a whole. A pro-patenting attitude is the basis of it. In other words, this attitude is being reflected by the fact that the social reputation for intellectual property is becoming higher in Japanese society.

As the social reputation of IP becomes higher through the pro-patenting attitudes permeating Japanese society at all levels, as evidenced in many other chapters of this book, the field of medicine is reflecting this trend. Medicine, as noted above, and medical practitioners who once were distanced from the rest of society because of high social status are coming again under scrutiny through the current phase of re-evaluation regarding IP. This is reflected in the current debates before the law courts which are redefining medical practices vis-à-vis industrial practices. In other words, in Japan medical treatment has not been seen historically to be compatible with commercialisation. Such debate has been reflected in the past year with reference to the selling of human tissue to create a human tissue bank for medical experiments. The production and selling of human tissue cells for this purpose has only recently been accepted under strict government guidance.[3] Therefore, the recent debates taking place in the Japanese law courts concerning the commercialisation of medical treatment, practice and body parts will have a great impact on the valuation of IP in relation to medicine. We look at the law courts' debates and decisions below.

Japanese patent law in relation to medicine

It is *not* written in the Japan Patent Law, but in the Patent Judge Standard that, in general, an invention which is industrially applicable applies to everything with only the following exceptions:

2.1 Exceptions

    (1)   Methods to operate, cure and diagnose human beings.
    (2)   Inventions which are not applicable to business.
    (3)   Inventions which are undoubtedly impossible.

    'Methods to operate, cure and diagnose human beings' refers usually to the operation, curing and diagnosis by medical doctors (or those instructed by medical doctors), and is therefore termed 'Medical Treatment'. 'Methods to operate, cure and diagnose human beings' does not apply to the methods to manage the extraction of anything from human beings or the methods to analyse them to collect data, but applies to the methods to managing them on the assumption that the same person will remain intact and whole due to medical treatment.

    'Methods to diagnose human beings' means the methods to collect data by measuring structures and functions of organs of the human body, and the methods to interpret the symptoms based on the above mentioned collecting methods.

    'Methods to operate, cure and diagnose animals' are regarded as 'Methods to operate, cure and diagnose human beings' unless the human being is clearly viewed as an exception to the object of the methods.

Case reports

Below are actual cases and their results with relation to what constitutes a form of medicine that can be subject to patenting:

April 11, 2002, Tokyo Court for Appeals
2000 (Gyo-Ke) 65 Patent Administrative Case
2000 (Gyo-Ke) 65 Patent Office Decision Abolition Appeals
Plaintiff: Surgical Navigation Technologies Inc.
Defendant: Director of the Patent Office
Judgement: Dismissed the appeal of plaintiff

The facts without debate
The procedure in the Patent Office
The name of the invention is 'The machine and the method to demonstrate an optical surgical operation repeatedly'

The reason for the Patent Office decision

The Patent Office recognised that this claim applies to the 'Method to diagnose human beings', meaning that the 'Method to diagnose human beings', is usually diagnosed by medical doctors (or those instructed by medical doctors), and therefore constitutes a 'Medical Treatment'. Thereby, it is applicable to Exception 2.1 (1) which means it is not an invention which is industrially applicable (Chapter 0.29).

The points of the Plaintiff Statement

It is an Error that 'Methods to diagnose human beings' ('Medical Treatment') lies within the 2.1 Exceptions to an invention which is industrially applicable:

(1) 'Industry' means the economical action of changing the form in order to create or enlarge the utility worth by adding human hands on natural items or the action of transfer, such as agriculture, stock farming, forestry, fishing, mining, manufacturing, commerce, trade, transport, traffic etc. Recently, 'Industry' is taken to be meant in a broad sense, so that finance and insurance are regarded as 'Industry'. It is unnatural that only 'Medical Treatment' is the exception of 'Industry'.

(2) Thought can be changed as time passes. What 'an invention which is industrially applicable' is and whether 'Medical Treatment' is 'an invention which is industrially applicable' or not should be judged as the present problem.

The points of the Defendant's Statement

It has been sustained with judicial precedent that one which essentially consists of the existence of the human body is not an invention which is industrially applicable (22 December 1970, Tokyo Court for Appeals, *Judicial Precedent Times*, Volume 260, page 334).

As the above mentioned judicial precedent shows, one which essentially consists of the existence of the human body, that is, 'Medical Treatment' should be regarded as the exception to 'Industry', and moreover, in the Patent Judge Standard, 'Methods to operate, cure and diagnose human beings' ('Medical Treatment') is not an invention which is industrially applicable.

Judgement of the Court

(1) 'Industry' is taken in a broad sense

'Industry', in general, has the meaning of work for production, that is, the economical action of changing the form in order to create or enlarge the utility worth by adding human hands on natural items or the action of transfer, such as agriculture, stock farming, forestry, fishing, mining, manufacturing, commerce, trade, transport, traffic etc. (*Kohjien*, 4th edition).

From the point of view of Patent Law (Chapter 11, Purpose), the purpose of this Law shall be to encourage inventions by promoting their protection and utilisation so as to contribute to the development of industry, in general, there is no reason why 'Industry' should not be taken in its narrow original sense.

(2) The existence of amendment precedent

The Japanese system has been maintaining the status quo regarding Medical Treatment, which states that techniques which relate to human existence and dignity and the techniques which are connected to such techniques are exceptions from being classified as patentable items, meaning pharmaceuticals, that includes their preparation methods, medicinal drinks and concoctions.

However, in 1975, with the Amendment Law 46, pharmaceuticals, their preparation methods, medicinal drinks and their concoctions became clearly under the protection of the patent, by removing them from exception status under patentable items (Patent Law 32).

(3) Open to everyone or not

The major grounds, mentioned above, of denying the patentability of medical treatment, that is, 'Medical Treatment should not be protected by the patent, but should be open to everyone, because Medical Treatment deeply relates to human existence and dignity', does not always incorporate sufficient power of persuasion.

If it relates to human existence and dignity and it is such an important technique that should be open to everyone, then the development of the technique should be promoted and protected by the means of a patent. In other words, it should be seen in terms of that 'it will be a larger contribution to human welfare in the final result'.

(4) Modern medicine (especially advanced medicine)

Modern Medical Treatment, especially advanced medicine, depends upon pharmaceuticals and medical devices, so that the choice of Medical Treatment is, in fact, under the control of patenting via pharmaceuticals and medical devices, even if the Medical Treatment itself has been made an exception from the patent.

It is worth noting the following standpoint; since it was decided that the techniques which relate to pharmaceuticals and medical devices are patentable, not only pharmaceuticals and medical devices but also the techniques which relate to Medical Treatment itself should be patentable as well as an invention which is industrially applicable, and there should be no reason to avoid this legally.

(5) Speciality of 'Medical Treatment'

However, there is a serious difference between pharmaceuticals and medical devices and Medical Treatment itself, determining the *raison d'être* for patentability. In the case of pharmaceuticals and medical devices, even if they are patented, it will not stop the medical doctors attempting to perform Medical Treatment to the best of their ability and using methods (pharmaceuticals and medical devices constitute the majority of them) to the best effect.

Although, in some situations, it may occur that some pharmaceuticals and medical devices which the medical doctor originally wants to use are prohibited because of a patent, it would only mean that the medical doctor would not be able to obtain them, but would not stop the medical doctor from performing the Medical Treatment. The medical doctor can do the Medical Treatment to the best of their ability using the best methods available without worrying about patenting.

In case of Medical Treatment only, it is different from above

In the case of Medical Treatment being patented, for the medical doctor who performs Medical Treatment, the possibility always exists that some of that Medical Treatment may be subject to patenting in any case.

Furthermore, in general, it is not always immediately clear whether a particular behaviour, on the part of the doctor would be subject to a patent right exercise or not, and it can be seen in this Court that it seldom occurs that claims are made concerning the infringement of a patent.

Medical doctors may perform Medical Treatment worrying that their methods or practices are subject to a patent infringement and subject to investigations. Medical doctors having to perform Medical Treatment with such a burden need to take countermeasures to cope with such circumstances, which may involve them in patenting themselves.

(6) Non-existence of fungible step

The system which drives medical doctors who perform Medical Treatment into such conflicting situations is remarkably unjust given the nature of Medical Treatment, and it would be a logical interpretation for Japan's patent system to not agree with such results.

Unless the Patent Law takes fungible steps to avoid such results, the Patent Law's position vis-à-vis Medical Treatment will remain unclear.

However, when the Patent Law allowed pharmaceuticals, their preparation methods, medicinal drinks and their concoctions to be subject to the protection of the patent, by removing them as exceptions from the patentable items, the following fungible step was accomplished; in relation to the patent of inventions concerning the preparation methods of pharmaceuticals, 'pharmaceuticals preparation methods which are prepared by the prescription slip written by medical doctors or dentists and pharmaceuticals which are prepared by the prescription slip written by medical doctors or dentists' are not outside of the validity of the patent (Patent Law 69 (3)). Yet, no fungible step was taken for the patent relating to Medical Treatment itself.

(7) Conclusion

In Patent Law, there are no concrete provisions that indicate whether general Medical Treatment is patentable. Therefore, as mentioned, it should be said there are no reasons that 'Industry' has to be interpreted narrowly. However, it should be noted there are no other interpretations defined by the Patent Law apart from the above mentioned reasons that inventions related to non-patentable Medical Treatment should be inventions defined as industrially applicable.

Although it is worth noting that as a legislative opinion, the Plaintiff statement that Medical Treatment itself should be patentable, this Court, as mentioned above, cannot agree with the interpretation of the Patent Law which does not include essential steps in order to allow patentability to occur.

Results from this case

The Court agreed with the Plaintiff on the following:
'Industry' should be taken in its broadest sense. Existence of an amendment precedent changed from non-patentable to patentable (pharmaceuticals, their preparation methods, medicinal drinks, and their concoctions). In the case of new techniques, developments should be promoted by patenting Advanced Medicine, contingent upon pharmaceuticals and medical devices being subject to a patent.

The Court disagreed with the Plaintiff on the following:
Special nature of 'Medical Treatment', that is, medical doctors should perform Medical Treatment to their best ability without any limitations or worry whether they are infringing a patent or not. There is no existence of a fungible step in Medical Treatment when the law was changed from non-patentable to patentable.

Confer

> U.S.: Medical Treatment: NOT an exception to Patent Law
> But, fungible steps exist. (U.S. Patent Law 287 (c) (1), 1996)
> Biotechnology Patents cannot be applied to this step.
> (U.S. Patent Law 287 (c) (2) A, 1996)

> EU: Medical Treatment: Exception of Patent Law (EPC 53 – (c))
> Adapted to WTO TRIPS 27 Paragraph 3 Previously, NOT industrially applicable
> (EPC 52–4), just in Japan.
> Japan: Medical Treatment: NOT industrially applicable
> Therefore, Not patentable.
> This case indicates the possibility of change in the future, will the reason change just as in the EU?

Future plan

Major premise

Both Patents and Medicine should be utilised for Human Beings especially in the case of improving the quality of life.

It is preposterous that Patents stop human lifesaving methods. Medical Doctors need to be allowed to operate to the best of their abilities without any limitations.

Borderline cases

Minor premise

1   Borderline cases of Advanced (patentable) and Ordinal (not patentable) Medicine
    Now the Japanese Government is planning to define Advanced Medicine as 'Biotechnology and/or regenerative medical techniques that takes place outside of the body'.

1   Borderline of Medical (patentable) and other (not patentable) treatment
2-1 Alternative medicine, such as Chinese herbal medicine
2-2 Cosmetic 2-3.

Sexual activity

2-1 A lot of universities and institutes are researching this
2-2 WHO QOL Psychological: Bodily image and appearance
2-3 WHO QOL Social Relations: Sexual activity.

However, do these borderline cases really qualify as Medical Treatment? Medical Treatment is usually supported by the national treasury because of the public health implications.

Notes

1   Acknowledgements: special thanks to Prof. Katsuya Tamai, Tokyo University, Prof. Yuichi Suzuki, Musashino Engineering University, Takuma Kiso, Mizuho Research Institute, Dr Ruth Taplin, Centre for Japanese and East Asian Studies.
2   This refers to the American Bayh-Dole amendment that promoted university–industry cooperation. See Terry A. Young's Chapter 2 in this book and Akio Nishizawa's slides in the Appendix for further elaboration.
3   See Ruth Taplin's article 'Therapy Focus: Medical Research using Human Tissues', *Bio People*, Winter 2002/3, Issue No. 4.

5 Intellectual property litigation, liability insurance, issues and solutions

Ian Lewis

Introduction

In this chapter, we will consider the insurance solutions[1] available to businesses which have spent inordinate amounts of time and money acquiring intellectual property rights. For solutions to arise there needs to be a better understanding of the risks involved with intellectual property litigation. It is important, therefore, to consider briefly the worth of intellectual property to a business; the potential threats to it, jurisdictional issues and the insurance cover available.

Importance of intellectual property to industry

Intellectual property (IP) represents the new currency of international business. This stems from the changing global economies, which are becoming more knowledge based. This has resulted in a major shift in business valuation, so that not only bricks and mortar (tangible assets) are included, but also those that are knowledge based (intangible assets). In 1978, 83 per cent of non-financial publicly traded firms' value was associated with their tangible assets, with 17 per cent associated with their intangible assets. By 1998, only 31 per cent of the value of the firms was attributed to their tangible assets, while 69 per cent was associated with the value of their intangibles.[2]

The value of IP rights is now an accepted part of a company's balance sheet. Indeed, accounting conventions have had to keep up to date with developments in this area, so that financial reporting standards now specifically deal with this aspect.[3]

IP rights are a cornerstone of many businesses. Their derived worth to a company is often a significant proportion, if not all, of their total assets. Financing strategies have evolved to use the value of the IP rights as security to finance and improve a business's short-term cash flow. A common pricing model to value IP has yet to be developed. Nonetheless, securitisation of IP is no longer a phenomenon; it is becoming part of every day asset use.

Like any asset of value, its protection should be an integral part of a company's risk management strategy, to minimise future loss and diminution in asset value. A loss of, or failure to secure full protection for, IP rights could have devastating financial implications to any business. Essentially, therefore, it is the value of the business that is at stake.

Exposures to business created by intellectual property

Varying intellectual property laws

The risks inherent in the ownership or use of IP for any business are similar worldwide. Regardless of where a business is domiciled, owners of IP rights face the same risks and exposures. However, what distinguishes the extent of the risk or the degree of the exposure is the owner's environment. For example, the rules and practices that regulate IP litigation procedures and remedies have been developed on a national basis with successful enforcement of rights or infringement liability being governed by, and dependent upon, the jurisdiction in which an action is brought.

There are international moves to harmonise IP laws and procedures. In Europe there is progress towards developing community-wide IP rights and a single community court. However, despite the success of the Community Trade Mark, the recent launch of the Community Design and pending Community Patent, it is often national courts that will decide upon validity or infringement issues, invariably leading to differences in interpretation of laws. In Japan, there have been tremendous changes in the IP systems and laws in order to bring them into line with other leading IP-reliant nations. Indeed, the Programme for Promoting the Creation, Protection and Exploitation of Intellectual Properties features the establishment of an Intellectual Property High Court and a law to ensure the prompt examination of patent applications.[4] Even the US has made changes to its IP laws and procedures, allowing publication prior to the granting of a patent and improved re-examination procedures.

A common goal seems to prevail, which is an attempt to reduce the period necessary to examine and dispose of IP disputes. In the United Kingdom, for example, the Woolf Reforms offer increased incentives for parties to avoid using the court system. The Civil Procedure Rules promote the use of Alternative Dispute Resolution (ADR) by providing that proceedings may be stayed pending ADR. Similarly, in Japan, efforts have been made to accelerate patent litigation proceedings. It took less than one month for the Tokyo District Court to grant preliminary injunction against the 'e-One' computer sold by Sotech, a Japanese company. Apple Computers had filed an unfair competition claim against Sotech on 24 August 1999 and the court issued the order on 20 September, after one hearing held on 14 September 1999.

However, regardless of the efforts to harmonise procedures, IP disputes are subject to national laws where differences in construction and intent still remain. This is exemplified by the fact that US patent law operates on a first to invent basis, whereas most of the rest of the world operates a first to file system.

Patent quality

One of the biggest problems facing industry is the issue of patent quality. It is often assumed that patents, once granted are novel and provide the owner with 'exclusivity' to the innovation for the life of the patent. This is, after all, the essence of the trade-off between business and state for the greater good. However, in recent times patent offices have had funding crises. They have struggled to recruit and retain qualified examiners at a rate commensurate with the massive increase in patent applications. In many cases, patent offices are being asked to be self-financing by their governments, to speed up the granting processes and reduce the backlog of applications. With such pressures upon examiners, their ability to conduct in-depth searches is diminishing rapidly.

It is in this crucial stage of patent search that the issue of novelty is often addressed, yet this appears to be the area suffering the most. Many organisations will be competing in the race to patent, often with two or more competing companies filing patents at or around the same time. Astonishingly, these patent applications will rarely be examined against each other. The publication process at least provides competitors with the opportunity to be aware of the potential for co-pending issues. However, in countries where there is no prior publication, the US[5] for example, the first you know of a competitor's patent is when it is granted. By this time, you may have invested millions of dollars in R&D or product sales and found yourself on the wrong end of a lawsuit.

Litigation costs

The costs incurred in IP litigation are high. As specialist knowledge is essential, there are a comparatively low number of experienced IP lawyers (*bendishi* in Japan) available. As a result, IP is one of the most expensive areas of law to litigate. The position with judges is even more acute, which has led some commentators to suggest that IP litigation can be a 'lottery' which depends on the judge hearing the case. In Japan, the Supreme Court wants to appoint 100 academics and engineers to assist judges when hearing complex IP trials.[6]

There are, however, dramatic variances in costs between jurisdictions. These variances are caused not just by the way IP rights are obtained, but also by the way the legal systems designed to resolve disputes operate. In Europe there are fundamental differences between legal systems. For example, the UK, where extensive discovery processes are often employed using a 'common law' legal system, it is considerably more expensive to litigate than, say, in the Netherlands or Germany, where 'codified laws' apply and legal costs are more controlled. In the US, they do not operate a 'loser pays' system, unlike most European countries. Therefore, the potential for imbalance, whereby large organisations 'freeze out' smaller opponents by escalating costs, is greater.

Not surprisingly, statistics show that the US is the most expensive of all jurisdictions. The average cost of patent litigation in the US is between $1.5m. and $2m. By comparison, the average cost in the UK is between US$0.5m. and $1m. Japan is considered to be no different to the UK. The cost of litigation in mainland Europe is unpredictable. In many jurisdictions, actions can be finalised for under US$50,000 where a summary judgement is made, but costs can rise significantly if actions proceed to trial. A good example of this is the Dutch 'Kort Gedding' procedure which often provides a fast and effective solution to many disputes.

Litigation costs are often not the key concern for many businesses. If a company is found to have infringed the rights of others, they may have to pay restitution in the form of civil damages. The levels of damages that are awarded vary greatly by jurisdiction. Most notably, the US has by far the highest levels of damage awards. The annual number of patent infringement awards/settlements in the US exceeding $15m. has doubled in the last five years.[7] Furthermore, patent infringement awards of $100m. or more are no longer uncommon.

By contrast, the awards of damages in other jurisdictions are not usually so high, although an award of US$27m. has been handed down by the UK courts. In Germany, one of the largest payments of US$29.1m. was made on 23 June 2003, to settle a long-running patent dispute between Honeywell and BorgWarner over turbochargers for cars.[8]

The following examples demonstrate the scale of awards that have been made:

Polaroid v. Eastman Kodak	$714m.
Eolas & University of California v. Microsoft	$520m.
Biogen v. Pharmacia	$141m.
Honeywell v. Minolta	$128m.
Stac v. Microsoft	$120m.
Fonar v. General Electric	$103m.

Need to enforce

Due to the value and competitive advantage IP rights afford, many organisations incur significant costs in registering patents, trademarks and designs and go to extreme lengths to establish their copyright. Unfortunately, some businesses will try to ride on the shirt tails of others by designing products or services as close to the original as possible. While this may be seen as fair business practice, some companies get too close and infringe the relevant patent, design or trade mark, thereby threatening the value of the right and reducing the returns to the owner of the rights.

The problem for the owner of the IP right is to stop the infringement. The inadvertent infringer will usually stop upon receipt of a 'cease and desist' letter from a lawyer. However, the determined infringer (or those who genuinely believe their product is different) will be much harder to stop. The IP right owner either has to negotiate or litigate to resolve the matter, and this will of course, be costly.

Failure to enforce such rights may be interpreted by others as a sign of weakness and encourage them to infringe as well, thereby compounding the loss in revenue or even threatening the very existence of the owner of the rights.

It is not unheard of for companies to undertake financial searches on small development companies to assess their ability to enforce their rights. If the small company appears financially weak, larger firms may blatantly copy their products, safe in the knowledge that they cannot afford to litigate. The experience from the UK market is that having appropriate insurance protection, and actively promoting it, is a good deterrent for would-be infringers.

Validity/ownership

Unfortunately, infringement is not the only risk facing the IP right owner. A challenge to the validity of the IP can be more devastating, and is becoming the favoured tactic of many. If a competitor can remove the 'monopoly position' afforded by the right concerned, they will have an open field to promote the same product or use the process. To the IP owner, this would mean the loss of all of their investment in R&D, trials or testing, marketing, tooling, etc., let alone the loss of future sales revenue. These sums can be vast, especially in fields such as biotechnology, pharmaceuticals or petrochemicals where development costs and subsequent profits are high.

There is a common misperception that, once granted, patents and other rights are set in 'tablets of stone'. This is not the case. They are vulnerable to attack on the grounds of invalidity, ownership or title. A competitor can even apply to the courts for a declaration of non-infringement to try to prevent the rights being enforced at a later date. In Europe, and Japan, opposition proceedings can be brought after grant of the patent by the respective patent office. Experience in Europe is that third parties often use opposition proceedings as a negotiating tool to commence licensing discussions. In the US there have been recent amendments to the re-examination process which, it is believed, will lead to more requests for re-examination.

But competitors are not the only parties that may challenge the ownership or validity of IP rights. The case of Joany Chou[9] is a good example of the type of action that can be brought by employees and researchers. In this case, Joany Chou was a graduate at the University of Chicago who alleged that her former supervisor, Prof. Roizman, intentionally failed to include her as an inventor on certain key patents around variants of the *Herpes simplex* virus. On 30 September 1999 she filed an amended suit against the University of Chicago and others claiming an assertion of inventorship, unjust enrichment, fraud, breach of fiduciary duty and various breaches of contract. This amended complaint seeks, among other things, monetary damages, correction of inventorship and ownership of the patents at issue, punitive damages, attorney's fees, costs and interest.

Infringement defence

Even if a company does not hold any IP rights, it may still have an exposure. All businesses are exposed to the risk of infringement of IP rights at one time or another. The exposure is increased if the company imports, manufactures, distributes, sells or even offers for sale a product or process. Somebody else's IP rights may protect all or part of the product or process. If they were to bring an action against an infringer, the infringing party would either have to agree a settlement or defend themselves through the courts. As shown, this can be very costly, especially if the defendant loses the case and is ordered to pay damages or a reasonable royalty. In 1991, Jerome Lemelson, an American, is reported to have collected over $100m. in licence fees mainly from Japanese companies he claimed breached his patents.

Additionally, an injunction may be obtained preventing the alleged infringing party from selling the product or using the process in future.

Undertaking in-depth searches of patent, trade mark or design registers prior to the development of a product or process is advisable. This is a good way of reducing exposure to actions by others, but does not guarantee non-infringement. There are so-called 'blind spots' where, for example, unpublished applications are not identified and furthermore, identification of copyright ownership is extremely difficult.

Exploitation agreements

Increasingly, companies are exploiting their IP through licence agreements, distributorship agreements, or transferring know-how and trade secrets via confidentiality and secrecy undertakings. These agreements are the tools through which many companies obtain tremendous wealth and control the use of their technology. Such agreements are often the result of many hours of negotiation and legal wrangling. The most common disputes arising from these agreements relate to non-payment of royalties, sales made outside agreed territories, or the enforcement of indemnity clauses agreed between the parties.

As awareness of IP exposures and fear of the cost of infringement liability increases, especially in the US, the use of IP indemnity clauses in contracts has risen dramatically. Such clauses used to be applied to life science or high technology companies, but today they are evident across many other sectors. Additionally, the trend towards outsourcing R&D is resulting in small companies having to indemnify large multinational organisations against patent or IP infringement disputes. In effect, this is David indemnifying Goliath, usually without adequate protection or the financial resources to do so.

This increased indemnity exposure is particularly prevalent in the IT sector where fears of infringing software and business method patents are a real concern. A current example is a Swedish-based company developing software for use in the mobile telecommunications sector, which has to defend a Swiss multinational in a US-based patent dispute. The costs for this case are estimated to be as high as $3m. with the potential damages exceeding $20m.

But indemnity obligations are not the only cause for dispute in IP-related agreements. A common problem can be non-payment of royalties or milestone payments. The loss of revenue to companies can be vast, especially if they are a non-commercial organisation. The case of *City of Hope National Medical Center v. Genentech*[10] is an example of where IP ownership or freedom of use is not in question, but the interpretation of the royalty element of the research agreement between them is. At trial, a jury awarded $300.1m. in compensatory damages for royalties that had not been paid and at a subsequent hearing a further $200m. in punitive damages to City of Hope Medical Center.

Many companies used to be able to rely on their normal insurance policies (e.g. professional indemnity or general liability) for such obligations linked to indemnity; however, this is no longer the case. Instead, companies have to seek specialist IP insurance in order to cover this increasingly onerous financial exposure. This change by the insurance markets is in direct response to the increased awareness of IP exposures, and the underwriters' need to properly and more suitably control this risk.

First-party Asset/Revenue Protection[11]

An often overlooked exposure to businesses is the direct financial loss that can result from an IP dispute. While the legal costs and damages can, themselves, be very high, the loss to a business is often compounded by the loss of opportunity or income.

Who is at risk?

Each company or business will have their own unique concerns about IP, be it the enforcement of their own rights, the risk of infringement of another person's rights, or both. Some may have large reserves to fall back on, others very little. However, the common theme throughout all of these concerns is the protection of the balance sheet.

Risk exposures vary greatly and are not restricted to the domicile of the business. Often, the exposure is determined more by where the business is trading, the sector of industry it operates within and the size of the business and its market share. Those trading in the US have the greatest risk of all, due mainly to the legal system and the general propensity for litigation. The size of a company can have a varying effect on exposure, with small businesses being more vulnerable to litigation costs, whereas larger firms can often withstand these. The industry sector is very important in determining exposure to IP risks as the following pie chart demonstrates (Figure 4):[12]

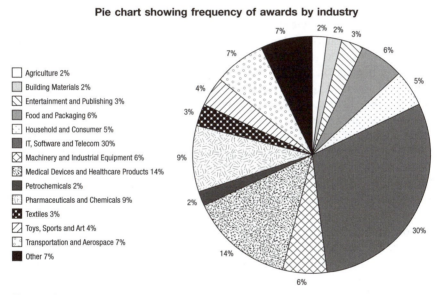

Pie chart showing frequency of awards by industry

- Agriculture 2%
- Building Materials 2%
- Entertainment and Publishing 3%
- Food and Packaging 6%
- Household and Consumer 5%
- IT, Software and Telecom 30%
- Machinery and Industrial Equipment 6%
- Medical Devices and Healthcare Products 14%
- Petrochemicals 2%
- Pharmaceuticals and Chemicals 9%
- Textiles 3%
- Toys, Sports and Art 4%
- Transportation and Aerospace 7%
- Other 7%

Figure 4

Source: Swiss Re, FSBG Patent Infringement Database.

Insurance solutions

Insurance cover for IP risks has developed considerably over the past few years despite there being fewer insurers willing to underwrite the class. At present, the scope of protection can be broad, but the number of insurers participating in the cover is low. However, this is predicted to change over time. At the time of writing, the number of insurers around the world that are actively involved in providing IP insurance as a regular product is no more than ten (counting all Lloyd's syndicates as one insurer).

It is interesting to note that there is much diversity between the types of insurance policy available in the key markets of Japan, the US and Europe. The US is the largest market in terms of premium income, with its focus being towards infringement defence policies. This is probably a result of their cultural environment, where a general fear of being sued prevails. Their legal system does not generally award costs to the losing party unless foul play has occurred. There is one company in the US that will consider providing offensive 'pursuit' cover, although their impact on the market is low at present.

The European markets are diversified, but easily come second in terms of overall premium. In fact, they are not far behind the US. The UK has been providing solutions for the longest period, in excess of 20 years. In overall premium terms, the UK is the largest of the EU markets, but Germany runs a close second. Other countries in which IP insurances are available include the Netherlands, Denmark and Sweden. The UK markets provide cover that is wider than is available elsewhere to clients worldwide. Access to Lloyd's can be obtained via a Miller facility and Lloyd's also provide support to the Swedish and Danish markets. The main interest in the UK market has traditionally been for pursuit cover, although there is growing demand for infringement defence, especially from companies trading in the US. The German market is predominantly a defence coverage market, at least at present.

The Japanese market is very limited with no known carrier actively promoting IP insurance, although some cover has been written by local carriers on a client-specific basis. However, the market is not dormant. One broker, Lead Insurance Services in Tokyo, has been working on solutions for the Japanese market and is able to source underwriting support in London. However, there are complications when sourcing support from London as it is necessary for local brokers/insureds to seek authority to utilise non-licensed carriers in the Japanese market. This is expected to change over time as the Japanese insurance market opens up further, and the awareness of insurance solutions increases among Japanese businesses.

Historically, IP insurance was purely a legal expenses policy (that solely covered legal costs involved in IP litigation) focused towards IP owners seeking to enforce their rights with low indemnity limits. Thus, many companies considered IP insurance to be of limited value. Increasing awareness of IP exposures has resulted in insurers expanding cover to meet client needs. In the UK there has been a gradual shift from indemnifying legal expenses only to including cover against damages if an action is lost. In the US the process has been different as most policies provide cover for damages automatically. Lately, protection for lost revenues or the value attaching to IP rights has been sought. Today, IP products range from litigation only policies, covering actions in the Netherlands solely, to world-wide infringement liability protection; US$50m. for large multinationals or revenue protection indemnities up to US$12m., for example. The insurance market remains open to further creative insurances in keeping with developing trends and client requirements. IP insurance is coming of age.

Notwithstanding the different types of cover, and ignoring subtle differences in the constitution of policies offered by insurers, a résumé of the key cover available is set out below.

Litigation and liability insurance

The main markets for these policies are in the UK and US, however, there are providers in other countries. There is no standard with policies covering all types of IP rights, for all forms of exposure worldwide, to those that cover defined rights in specific territories.

Because of the differences in national laws, incidence and severity of litigation and liability around the world, the scope of cover available will vary, but in general it can be obtained for the following:

Pursuit: Professional fees and expenses incurred in pursuing those who infringe IP rights. Cover can apply to virtually all forms of IP right, from patents to copyright, from trade marks to trade secrets and domain names.

Defence: Professional fees and expenses incurred in defending a claim by a third party that the products or processes used by the Assured infringe IP rights of others. Policies often include cover for damages or agreed settlements.

Invalidity: Professional fees and expenses incurred in defending a challenge to the ownership, validity or title to IP rights. Cover can include post-grant opposition actions in the European Patent Office and Japanese Patent Office as well as interference and re-examination actions in the US.

Agreements: Professional fees and expenses and, in some cases, damages incurred when honouring indemnity clauses in an agreement. In certain cases, cover can also apply for professional fees and expenses incurred when enforcing the contractual terms of an agreement.

Virtually all policies operate on a 'claims made' basis, which means that they only cover matters that the Insured becomes aware of, and notifies underwriters about during the currency of the policy. Matters that may give rise to a dispute before the cover is incepted, or that are notified after the policy has expired, are usually excluded. Some policies require the Insured to utilise panel counsel, and others do not. In the European Union, there is a directive stipulating that the Insured should have the freedom to select their representative, although this may not apply if damages cover is provided.

An example of a dispute supported by underwriters in London applies to a European-based company which developed an enhanced form of communication device. The company had filed many patent applications in most industrialised countries, and had raised substantial investment from public offerings and licensing arrangements. The company and some of its licensees received unsubstantiated threats of infringement from a business in the US. This caused concern for the licensees, who had requested to be indemnified from such issues as per the terms of their licence agreement. Despite numerous, and at times long-winded, attempts to settle the matter, it became apparent that this was not proving successful. Having received advice from leading IP lawyers, the insured, with support from insurers, filed for a declaration of non-infringement in the US courts. The estimated cost of running the declaratory judgement action to completion is more than $2m.

First-party Asset/Revenue Protection insurance

IP asset protection insurance complements the cover provided by litigation and liability insurance. Asset/Revenue Protection policies are designed to protect the revenue streams generated by IP rights. This form of coverage is relatively new to the market but holds great potential as a way of securing the investments made in IP by industry. This form of coverage will become the equivalent of property insurance for intangible assets.

This new form of IP Insurance is explored more fully by Matthew Hogg in Chapter 6 entitled, 'Protection of intellectual property value/revenue and the insurance solution'.

Who should consider intellectual property litigation and liability insurance?

In short, most companies should investigate the suitability of IP insurance to them, as virtually all businesses are exposed to IP rights in their daily operations. Evidence has shown that the existence of an IP litigation and liability policy acts as an effective deterrent to litigation. It often accords the insured the financial muscle to force their opponent to concede to early settlement. Clearly, companies with limited resources, particularly new ventures or, indeed, those wanting to protect their balance sheet position should consider this insurance.

Historically, it was only small enterprises wanting to be able to fund the enforcement of their rights, which considered this form of cover. However, following improvements to the policies available, litigation and liability insurance is now purchased by a whole host of businesses and organisations. There has been a boom in the number of companies looking for 'defence' cover as a method of supporting their 'freedom to operate', or as a requirement under a licence or distribution type agreement. Some large multinationals have tailored cover to suit elements of their operation or subsidiary businesses. Universities and research organisations concerned about enforcement costs or contractual indemnities also purchase cover. Even venture capitalists have sought cover for their investee companies.

Future developments

There are numerous developments taking place in the insurance market. Certainly, insurers are gaining a better understanding of IP exposures and risk assessment techniques. The improvement in the insurance climate will result in more carriers coming into this field, and competition will fuel product diversification and enhancement.

As industry and the economies of the developed world increasingly understand the value of IP, there will be increased demand for suitable IP insurance covers. It is interesting to note that the European Commission is evaluating the potential advantages of creating a pan-European patent insurance to fund litigation risks for European nationals. It will be intriguing to find out if this is something that other governmental bodies investigate.

Summary

The increase in awareness of IP rights and the value they bring to industry is increasing at an alarming rate. Governments are striving to create new laws to support and protect their industrial base in the burgeoning knowledge economy. In addition, the question of patent quality is being addressed, albeit slowly.

At the same time, the traditional professional support services are responding to the challenges and issues that this dramatic shift in business process is creating. Led by the legal and patent attorney professions the financial support services of accountancy and insurance are fast becoming alive to the opportunities of embracing these changes. It could be said that the insurance industry is behind all of the other professions in understanding IP exposures, but this will not be the case for very long. As the insurance markets turn the corner of the difficult general market conditions that prevail at present (and they will) IP insurance will become a fundamental part of any risk management programme.

That said, insurance solutions already exist and through IP insurance businesses can increase their financial security to support their innovation and investment in the future.

Notes

1 The above review is not entirely comprehensive and should only be considered as a guide. Full terms and conditions including the respective insurance policies should be obtained in order to fully understand the coverage. If in doubt, always seek clarification or advice from a specialist insurance intermediary.

2 Dr Margaret Blair, Brookings Institution, quoted in Julie L. Davis and Suzanne S. Harrison *Edison in the Boardroom: How Leading Companies Realize Value from their Intellectual Assets* (2001). New York: John Wiley & Sons.
3 Explored further in Chapter 6.
4 New Court is a feature of Japanese IP reforms – Ralph Cunningham – Legal Media Group – 13 July 2003.
5 It is acknowledged that the USPTO now operates a publication process.
6 Source: Legal Media Group – 30 August 2003.
7 Source: Swiss Re, FSBG Patent Infringement Database.
8 Source: Lessons in litigation – from Lego bricks to LED's – *Managing Intellectual Property* – July/August 2003. Euromoney Plc.
9 *Joany Chou v. the University of Chicago, ARCH Development Corp, Bernard Roizman and Aviron* – 8 July 1999.
10 Source: Christopher Thornham, 'A $500 million question – US damages award to City of Hope National Medical Center in royalties dispute with Genentech', *European Biopharmaceutical Review* – Autumn 2002: 50–2.
11 See Chapter 6.
12 Source: Swiss Re, FSBG Patent Infringement Database.

6 Protection of intellectual property value/revenue and the insurance solution

Matthew R. Hogg

Background

The time has come for global business to truly take account of the value of its intellectual property and, for that matter, all its intangible property. In the last 10 to 15 years there has been a patent race, particularly seen in the US, as industries woke up to the potential benefits of exclusive rights. The acknowledgement and clarification of intellectual property matters has, in this time, been recognised by the World Trade Organisation, and reform of IP cross-boundary rights was again highlighted in the TRIPS agreement.[1] Yet, once these rights are obtained there appears to be the misunderstanding that they are indestructible and their value assured. Those who understood the importance of IP value often failed to take those final steps to safeguard and protect it.

It is worth commenting in this chapter that new pressures will come to bear upon key decision-makers within business, forcing their hand on the issues of intellectual property valuation and financial risk assessment. The latest influences started just a few years ago, but the future holds yet more in store.

Surprisingly, CEOs around the world may benefit, however, from the forward momentum that IP valuers and the insurance industry can provide. Their impetus might prove the saving-grace for executives from the anxious and bemused stakeholder.

How the world has changed

'Science knows no country, because knowledge belongs to humanity, and is the torch which illuminates the world' – such were the innocent words of one Louis Pasteur before the years of globalisation and booming competition. We have heard this sentiment linked to the concept of rewarding innovation today for the prospect of further discovery tomorrow, but it possibly stretches our imagination to think that this was Pasteur's humble opinion.

The world has changed radically in the last century in the face of technological advances, commercialisation and globalisation. Although there are still a number of inventors, academics and scientists who still believe in discovery for discovery's sake, they are too frequently eaten up by the corporate animal intent on discovery for profit's sake. This has led to that 'knowledge economy', of which Ian Lewis speaks in Chapter 5 of this book. Management gurus are quick to point out that the economy of days gone by was built on land, labour and capital. It is not the case that these possess little value today, but rather that it has become normative to push the boundaries of doing more with less. Diminished land resources, decreased importance of labour and all at a cheaper price is the way of the world now. Financial value and, consequently, commercial demands are now placed upon our ideas and intellectual capital as they distinguish us from the opposition and drive up our success or share price. Science, for one, very rarely finds itself in the hands of society but in the hands of the global corporate, as any opponent to patenting life forms or naturally occurring substances will tell you.

Recognition of the value in IP protection

In recent years industry has realised the benefits of gaining intellectual property rights, with the strategy that if enough are applied for there will always be a few that are commercially viable and maintain a market lead. An obvious example of this behaviour could be seen in the Hewlett-Packard 'invent' campaign which started in December 1999 and, by providing financial incentives to employees, saw its patent applications nearly double by 2001.

This trend of increased patent application filings can be seen globally. The last Trilateral Statistical Report in 2001 showed the rapid rise in applications globally at about 25 per cent from just 1996 to 2000, with the US application filings at around 48 per cent (see Figure 5). This trend seems set to continue despite the rather shaky global economy, and recent statistics show increases of around 25 per cent in 2002 from 2000.[2]

The mass of Japanese patent applications does not necessarily indicate that Japanese industry is inventing at a much higher rate or recognising patent value beyond that of their global competitors. There are a number of reasons that might explain this dynamic, such as the fact that, until recent years, patents in Japan have had to be filed very narrowly in scope, resulting in a number of patents to cover one area. Although there is now the ability to gain a patent on a broader scope, many companies are probably still working on their old patent strategy. The cost of obtaining patents in Japan is also much less than the European average.

Despite increasing patent applications, the problem remains, however, that, once the company has received its portfolio of patents or other IP, it tends to forget that unless time, effort and strategy are spent on the 'creation' it becomes only as valuable as the paper the right is printed on.

World-wide Patent Applications

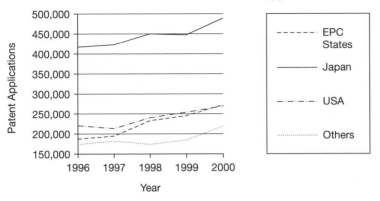

Total World-wide Patent Applications

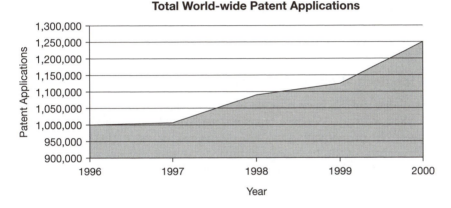

Figure 5

Also, in this state of inertia, there develops a belief that the IP owner is untouchable by others because of their 'exclusive' grant of rights. Although there is understanding of the value of obtaining patents there has been poorer comprehension that these intangible assets should obtain the same treatment as other tangible assets within the business. The significant effects of this attitude are that direct or indirect value from these rights is lost and the protection of that value is barely considered.

Intangible assets should be treated as assets

The importance of competitive products has obviously existed since the origins of trade. It has become all the more necessary and lucrative to obtain a whole host of intellectual property rights within that product to ensure some degree of control in the market and to differentiate from competitors. We have not seen an approach by management in many industries to segregate the 'product' from its intrinsic IP rights so as to identify separate and distinct risks to protect the business viability and success. There appears to be a frequently recurring belief that all IP-associated risks are business risks that either succeed, bringing in revenue to the company (making it successful) or fail, so that another idea must be brought forward. It is, however, much more complicated if one considers the precarious state of the patent system and that the 'goodwill' of the company and its brands are often engendered by the intellectual capital of its workers and products.

To fully understand the capacity and totality of a corporate entity is to fully accommodate the wealth of intangible property that it incorporates and its effective financial value. This value should then be protected by all means necessary from those risks threatening its fruition, and should include sound legal diligence and appropriate risk management. The health and vitality of the business is at stake, let alone the true determination of its worth. It is now legendary that IBM manages to realise around $1.5 billion in licensing revenue from its intellectual property rights, but not all IP value is quite so transparent to the stakeholder or even the board member. That value is also rarely protected by insurance.

The intellectual property insurance evolution

Pressure has always been brought to bear on the insurance industry to face up to the issues that concern business, and Lloyd's of London has been at the forefront of innovative insurance cover since its origins in the seventeenth century. With the change in business over the recent years has come a new threat to the assets of the company. Indeed, as we have seen, not only have ideas and 'intangible property' become a global currency, but they have been only recently redefined as the vast majority of an organisation's assets.

Although some might say that the awareness of IP value to the company is still in a transition stage, it is more frequently making headline news and gaining the attention of both Chief Executives and company Risk Managers. In the last ten years or so there have been around three dozen patent lawsuits or settlements topping $100 million each let alone the hundreds of other cases which have significantly hit companies' 'bottom lines'.[3] Awards such as the most recent of $521 million against Microsoft[4] make for worrying headlines and force business to challenge the way they utilise their potentially fragile and hugely important assets. This presents great challenges in terms of evaluation and protection and that means, or at least it should mean, the provision of insurance.

In the last few years, surveys by both the Association of Insurance and Risk Managers (AIRMIC) and other insurance bodies have highlighted the recent fears for business. Not long ago, fire would still have been the main cause of concern, but the typical top three greatest risks facing businesses are now more likely to be viewed as:

1   Business interruption
2   Loss of reputation
3   Products liability/tamper/brand protection.[5]

This shows the keen interest within risk management circles of the value and risk within intangibles. When you consider that intellectual property risk often features in the top ten and reputation and brand are often bound up with trade mark issues the problem becomes clear. Realistically, it is often only within the powers of board members to analyse and budget for intellectual property valuation and protection rather than the risk-savvy insurance manager.

The initial insurance products to help protect the intellectual property value in a company have proved of value to a certain niche of firms, and are often tangential to the buyer's real concerns over their IP. These first policies provided legal expenses cover and liability cover to insure against any damages that may be incurred as a consequence of such litigation being lost.[6] It has only been in the last couple of years that basic first-party-loss principles have been applied to the new risk environment.

Protecting value with first-party IP insurance

In the days before the 'knowledge economy', protections from first-party losses were developed to satisfy the wants of industry, thus shielding it from excessive impacts to the main drivers of its revenue. Such policies allowed the insureds to financially recoup losses resulting from damage to buildings or machinery. Protecting oneself from losses enables the freeing of financial restraints and encourages development. Interestingly, Mehr and Cammack in their book *Principles of Insurance* believed that the rise of Great Britain in the nineteenth century as a great trading nation and its solid fire insurance amenities during that time were no coincidence. As economies lag a little and capital investment and R&D input lessens in high-tech industry this may be worth digesting. As will be discussed later, the comfort derived from passing risk to a third party can improve trade and encourage entrepreneurs.

A first-party insurance policy allows a company to protect the commercial value of its intellectual property rights in the same way as it would insure its headquarters, plant or stock with a fire policy. The value of the IP can be attributed to the future sales of products to which it forms an integral part or could, alternatively, be the R&D or financial investment that has been incurred. In the latter case, it may be possible to insure the actual investment made or, depending on the circumstances, the anticipated royalties or equity in the IP. Depending on the breadth, depth and quality of intellectual property, the entirety of the company's IP may be insured or, more commonly, a select portfolio of intellectual property. That portfolio should include those rights with the greatest strategic importance or value.

As all IP policies are underwritten on a bespoke basis to suit the particular requirements of each portfolio it is also possible to design a policy to effectively cover the costs of implementing a contingency plan should there be an inability to exploit the IP. This can be particularly effective for companies that regularly release new products or provide products that are difficult to quantify and value. In such circumstances the insurer promises to pay those costs necessary to speed up the insured's ability to bring the next IP project to fruition.

The core risk to the realisation of IP revenue returns is arguably that of a third-party action or, possibly, an employee or ex-employee successfully challenging the IP rights through the usual legal forums. This would typically be the case of an unsuccessful defence of an infringement action or a finding of invalidity of the rights in whole or in some aspect. The most dramatic loss might, therefore, be in the event of a loss of a patent right and a corresponding loss of monopoly in the market, or even having to withdraw from that market entirely. In the case of having to share a market with competitors or holders of stronger IP, it may be that anticipated earnings have been reduced due to the necessity to purchase a licence and/or the effect of royalty payments.

Other risks that might be advisable to cover are, first, actions by government or states that either remove the IP right or limit its financial exploitation, and second, any adverse or misleading media reports that highlight an undesirable quality in the intellectual property or brand. While appearing to be of secondary importance to the effects of successful legal challenge, the coverage for loss due to government action has become a hot topic. Although there are small-scale actions stifling exploitation of IP rights on a regular basis, it is only the larger examples that gain media attention. Situations such as the attitude of African countries towards the 'Aids patents'[7] or the recent announcement of the real brains behind the depth-charge[8] of Second World War fame should provide food for thought.

Valuation in first-party IP insurance

As previously indicated, the purpose of designing first-party IP cover has been to provide an insurance policy to work in much the same way as existing tangible property coverage. There should, theoretically, be little to differentiate the insurability of a tangible asset and that of an intangible asset with an insurable interest. A few insurers have tried, and unfortunately failed, in this arena by using complex alternative risk transfer mechanisms. There is no obvious need for this choice if the parameters of the insurance are well structured.

The issue of IP valuation is one that many experts are still coming to terms with and it seems that it may not be possible for some time to obtain a structure that satisfies the accountants as well as IP owners and their lawyers. Those in the know will talk of leading methodologies such as valuation on a cost, market or income basis but at all times it is important to recognise and apply some degree of flexibility to the rules depending on the particular intellectual property being valued. While insurers will utilise valuation experts in transactions, what is of paramount importance is defining the value of the IP to be insured prior to the agreement of the cover and to ensure that such values are stated in the insurance contract. This will avoid unnecessary post-loss dispute. The potential insured is bound to have his or her own opinion as to the value of the assets but although there may be some flexibility in agreeing financial sums up front, the current uncertainty over IP valuation methods will prove deadly to any valuation agreement undertaken at a time of loss.

It is now common practice to build into the insurance contract defined values for each particularly valuable piece of IP and also to understand the 'split' of the value over the particular years of indemnity in the contract. At present, the intellectual property is linked to the product from which it typically derives its value, and the dependency of each piece of IP within that product is considered separately. This may prove to be of varying difficulty to establish depending on the product itself. A pharmaceutical drug may well only be formed from a handful of patents and trade marks, yet a vital but one of many patents incorporated into a car engine may be trickier to value if the manufacturer of the part does not license the technology to another.

There are still strides that can be made in the field of valuation and intellectual property coverage, but business should be encouraged that at least there is now an insurance industry response to the calls of concern over the threat of intellectual property exposures.

External pressures to protect with IP insurance

There is, and will continue to be, an enthusiasm for IP valuation and insurance products for many more reasons than the fact that IP rights are a fundamental cornerstone to the modern economy. The simplistic view, and one that holds great weight, is that IP owners are slowly beginning to see the prospect of being able to protect one of the most significant assets of their business. It has taken some time and, to date, insufficient attention has been given to intangible risk matters, either by business or the insurance markets. As a matter of urgency, business must assess its own potential weaknesses and set about effective management for the protection of IP. The very real threats to market value and financial return must be evaluated and recovery plans orchestrated. Business must also consider whether the potential financial instability caused by the residual threats to intangible assets should be carried by the business or passed to an insurer.

There is now a flurry of external pressures on industry to turn their attention not only to the safekeeping of their IP but also to value it correctly as a true and fair reflection of the company itself. These driving forces include increasing corporate governance standards, national accountancy changes and the current state of the economy.

The role of corporate governance

One of the most powerful drivers of change to be felt throughout the board-room and implemented to the grass roots of companies is the emergence of higher standards of corporate governance. Although there has, for a few years now, been discussion and encouragement at national levels for strong corporate responsibility to all stakeholders, the events surrounding such fiascos as Enron, Andersen and WorldCom have shifted all expectations and attitudes. A far more elevated public understanding has heightened the expectancy of a sound corporate ethos and accountability to shareholders.

We are not talking about delving into the realms of corporate social responsibility here, but rather the economic responsibilities of the firm. However, if we consider that business reflects its value to stakeholders and the general public in terms of intangibles such as IP and reputation it must ensure that it has implemented policy in order to effect sound practice and build a complimentary perception. It is time for companies, in many fields of practice, to go beyond mere compliance and to consider their business practice in wholly new ways.

In the coming years we can, therefore, expect a greater degree of delib-erated consideration given to all risks that a business might run, given the requirements of corporate transparency and thorough risk evaluation. In this process of identifying, analysing and controlling risks to the business we can expect the dependency upon intangible property to be thrust into the limelight. As discussed later in this chapter, we would also expect that after quantifying all residual risk, when all other means to minimise or eliminate it have been exhausted, it must be considered whether the trans-ferral to a third party by way of insurance is appropriate. The availability of first-party insurance coverage for intellectual property will become invaluable.

International accounting changes

Another catalyst demanding recognition of intellectual property risk will be the international accountancy changes currently being discussed and those that have been implemented. The International Accounting Standards are driving us forward, yet a number of countries have already seen their accounting provisions altered in an effort to form a globally common expression of all the assets of a company.[9] Having previously been loaded in favour of tangible assets, goodwill and IP are now appearing on balance sheets to attempt to provide a truer reflection of the company's assets. These values are then subject to the process of amortisation in the financial reports and accounts.

We can expect a higher degree of sophistication in accounting standards and in the valuation of intangible assets in the future as intangibles are given the attention they deserve. Board directors will have to exercise their choice of strategy, risk profiling and risk transfer as the relevance and acknowledgement of intellectual property is raised.

Diminishing venture capital funds and R&D expenditure

The current economic climate, that some might say shows little signs of being a 'dip' in the cycle but rather an adjusted and settled 'base' following global events, is conducive to the development and desirability of intellectual property valuation, protection and intellectual property insurance. Evidence has shown diminishing venture capital investment, banking finance and internal research and development expenditure through much of industry. Particularly heavily hit have been the bio-tech, pharmaceutical and hi-tech fields as, increasingly, start-ups and 'think-tanks' are competing for less venture capital funds or other investment; the larger institutions are frequently needing to cut back their R&D expenditure due to the tightening of purse-strings.[10]

In the competition for investors, smaller companies are given the opportunity to set themselves apart from the crowd if they hold intellectual property insurance. By protecting the expected revenue streams of the IP rights, or the investment itself, from deterioration due to associated IP risks, the investor is given confidence in their outlay. Indeed, the underwriting process, with its legal and financial audit, suggests to the capital provider that this IP has been scrutinised and found satisfactory by lawyers, accountants and interested third parties.

Although an insurance policy will not underwrite the IP 'idea' itself nor the competency of its owners, one of the significant risks, that of losing the IP rights in court, can be reduced in severity. The benefits of this can be used to encourage the banking industry whose loans to IP-rich companies may well be constrained by the amount of collateral in the tangible sense. The IP valuation fears of the bank may well be satisfied by the report of the auditors involved and the strength of the intellectual property rights as examined by lawyers. Additionally, the insurance of intellectual property should become a viable comparison to the insurance of tangible property when offering a loan, for example an agreement to purchase insurance on a property prior to the agreement of a mortgage.

By assisting companies in enhancing the acceptability of their IP as collateral to a loan or as a strong financial earner, financing should become a little easier for companies large and small. The larger companies may find that they can influence alternative and more efficient methods of financing, while a venture capital prospect might find itself being an ideal investment opportunity. Regardless, it makes sound economic sense to protect the future revenue streams of the entity and free up capital for further use such as R&D investment.

Closing thoughts

In the coming years we will see an increasing pressure subjected upon IP-rich owners to protect their financial position and contemplate aspects of risk that were not readily considered 20 or 30 years ago. Shareholders and investors are becoming ever more demanding of thorough risk assessment and an accurate portrayal of businesses' true assets at a realistic and determinable level. Current political, accounting and economic conditions will drive both the valuation of IP and risk awareness.

What may be a little slower to circulate is the realisation that the insurance industry is now making a genuine effort to give companies, which perceive benefits in doing so, the ability to share the risks involved. Additionally, the new first-party cover can provide links to valuation experts and should aid in the realisation of further financial investment and securitisation. This will be to the benefit of all business groups and industries, as the market has already seen, with Global 500 companies to venture capital groups and start-up initiatives all seeking coverage.

Notes

1 Trade-Related Aspect of Intellectual Property Rights, negotiated in the 1986–1994 Uruguay Round introduced intellectual property rules into the multilateral trading system.
2 International PCT patent application filings up from 90,948 in 2000 to 114,048 in 2002.
3 Personal database of IP large losses based on media and company reports in the last 15 years.
4 University of California and Eolas Technologies brought suit against Microsoft for plug-in and applet patents violated by use within Microsoft's Internet Explorer browser and in August 2003 a jury found Microsoft liable to the sum of $521 million.
5 The Aon European Risk Management and Insurance Survey 2002–3.
6 See Chapter 5 in this book by Ian Lewis.
7 After continual negotiation over the threat of infringement of Aids patents for reasons of public safety and health, the latest news in August 2003 is the Brazilian government's announcement that it will infringe the Roche patent on 'nelfinavir'.
8 A collection of letters, papers and photographs has recently been uncovered in the UK regarding the invention of the depth-charge, used successfully during the Second World War, by Herbert Taylor and the legal battle as the US decided to ignore the usual protocol of intellectual property rights.
9 For example, FRS 10 and 11 in the UK or SFAS 141 and 142 in the US.
10 For example, the Ernst and Young's European Biotechnology Report 2003 highlights that the amount of investment in European biotech companies has fallen from €6.7 billion in 2000 to just €1.2 billion in 2002. It also shows a resulting drop in R&D expenditure within public companies of around 18 per cent, and an industry average decrease of 6 per cent.

7 Standardisation and patent pools in Japan

Their effects on valuing IP and limits under competition law

Masako Wakui[1]

1 Introduction

The value of a patent largely counts when a patent technology becomes a standard that is used widely in the industry. It is possible for a holder of a patent right to acquire a huge licence fee from many licensees under several circumstances. This includes such circumstances where a certain standard has to be adopted to make a patent a product and where a certain patent technology has to be used for this purpose. Recently, many companies are pursuing the strategy that in general a standard is established to favour their companies and, in particular, that their patent technology, if possible, is incorporated into a standard.

The relationship between this technology standard and a patent causes two types of problems. First of all, there is a possible danger that a technology standard is placed under the control of a patent right holder, who may abuse his position. Under such control, some problems may arise from an action taken by a patent holder; one example is that the price of a product that adopted a technology standard may soar and another is that other companies are excluded from the market as a result of being refused a patent licence, which is tantamount to denying use of a technology standard.

Second, another problem that may arise is that the standardisation of a technology is prevented or distorted. There are concerns that a standard may not prevail fully as other companies may not be willing to adopt the standard because of concerns such as an abuse of position by a right holder, obligation to pay a high licence fee and prolonged time spent on the licence negotiations. Added to this is the concern that the process of standardisation is prevented or distorted as companies may seek only their own profits with a view to gaining possible higher licence fees. This issue is becoming serious both as a great number of patents begin to cover a standard and as the importance of the patent begins to be recognised to a higher degree.

A patent pool is a licence scheme which is attracting attention as being a medium to solve these problems. A patent pool enables a one-stop shopping arrangement under the systematised control of various licences and it has the function to realise that a licence fee is contained within an appropriate amount in total. These functions are evaluated highly as being able to resolve many problems regarding a standard and a patent.

However, patent pools may cause another series of problems. In some cases, patent pools may enable parties to avoid competition and determine higher licence fees. A patent pool may abuse its status and exclude competitors. These concerns raise the need for effective regulation for a patent pool under competition law. A patent pool has to be formed and operated without violating the rules of competition law. There are, indeed, some cases of patent pools regulated under Japanese competition law – antimonopoly law. Therefore, what are the regulations set by antimonopoly law? Or what should they be?

In this section, first of all, we will introduce the details of the problems regarding standardisation, the patent and the patent pool. Then, an analysis is made regarding what kinds of functions the patent pool that collected patents in relation to a standard technology realises from the point of view of impact on the market. It will be explained that one of the main important functions is the evaluation of patent value and the lowering of a total patent fee. At the same time, we will consider the negative aspects such as the raising of a licence fee. This is followed by an analysis of how the antimonopoly law sets a limitation on this type of patent pool. After analysing the related guidelines as well as the empirical case studies, we will assess rules and expected outcomes, by referring to the above analysis as well as cases and arguments abroad.

2 Standard patent pools and problems

Standards are defined as documented technical specifications or other precise criteria to be used consistently as rules, guidelines, or definitions of characteristics, to ensure that materials, products, processes and services are fit for their purpose.[2] Standardisation involves setting such standards in order to unify or simplify technical aspects of goods or services (hereafter collectively 'goods'), which otherwise tend to be diverse, complicated or disorderly. Standardisation among firms, types of goods or countries widens the market, enabling economy of scale and more varieties that benefit consumers as well as firms. Standards also function to convey the information that the goods have sufficient quality, which promotes new entry into different markets.[3] Standardisation is particularly important for information communication technology because its usefulness depends on interconnectivity with other networks, equipment and services, and standardisation is a precondition for this. Against these backgrounds, and with the additional factor that the life-cycle of goods is getting shorter, customers sometimes postpone buying until standards are established widely in the market to avoid the risk of being locked into later obsolete technologies that cannot be used with other goods. Companies are, therefore, actively trying to establish standards.

There are various ways to set standards. Formal standard bodies such as the ISO (International Organization for Standardization), ITU (International Telecommunication Union), CEN (the European Committee for Standardization) or JISC (Japanese Industrial Standards Committee) set a 'de jure standard'. The so-called 'de facto standard' is the one set by way of voluntary coordination among firms or by a single firm's effort to make their own technology predominate, a prominent example of which is Microsoft Windows.

A patent matters in standardisation because it may hinder standard setting, implementation and promotion. Patent owners may refuse the licence and block competitors from introducing the standard. They may charge a high royalty to licensees which also hinders standards dissemination. The possibility of abuse or high profit can distort the process of standardisation as potential patent owners have incentives to implement their proprietary technologies into the standards. The earlier standards are established, the more standards are covered by patents. And as the standards become more important, the risk of abuse increases. Standardisation is confronting the need to control the exercise of patent rights.

Where a strong position exists in the technology market there is room for abuse in terms of the stifling of competition. The patent's standardisation blocking effect is also a cause for concern in this regard, for it may impede the development of competition. Though the diffusion of a standard does not always benefit the public – as it may have effects such as reducing diversity, diminishing competition through facilitating coordination or exclusion of innovative goods – standardisation can have a significant positive effect, being a precondition of the very existence of competition. To the extent that standardisation promotes competition, its distortion represents an obstacle to competition. Regulation of abusive conduct promotes competition in this way too. Furthermore, limiting the possibility for abuse is desirable in preventing potential patent owners from endeavouring to distort the process of standardisation.[4]

The patent system is meant to promote innovation. Promoting innovation benefits consumers and also competition because it promotes competition. Therefore, the task is twofold: we need to regulate patent owners' conduct so that they do not distort the standardisation process and competition, but we have to do it without hindering innovation through sacrificing the effectiveness of the patent system.

There are several ways to solve the problem, such as compulsory licensing[5] and setting rules through standardisation bodies.[6] Collecting patents into a pool and licensing in a non-discriminatory manner under a reasonable, preset term is one such way and has, indeed, been introduced, especially in the IT field.

The Radio Corporation of America (RCA), organised in 1919, is a pioneering case. Major manufacturers such as General Electronics, Westinghouse, Marconi and AT&T pooled their patents relevant to transatlantic radio communication systems at its formation and, later, patents relevant to TV equipment, which included the patents that were needed to be licensed for implementation of the Federal Communications Commission (FCC) standards.[7]

A recent notable case is the MPEG-2 patent pool, which collects patents essential for implementation of a series of MPEG-2 Video and Systems standards (ISO/IEC (the International Electrotechnical Commission) 13818-1 and 2). The patent owners agreed to license a licensing organisation, MPEG-LA, to sub-license their technologies, and under the licences MPEG-LA offers a non-discriminatory licence package on preset terms. Since its launch in 1994, the portfolio has grown to include more than 550 patents worldwide, owned by over 20 companies. The patent owners come from the US, Europe, Korea, Japan and so on. Their core business also varies from communication services to universities. The organisation provides licences to more than 500 firms all over the world.[8] Other pioneering projects are DVD6C[9] and DVD3C[10] which offer necessary licences, each promoting DVD (Digital Versatile Disc) standards. They are relatively small pools, consisting of only seven companies (6C) – four of which are Japanese companies, and three other companies (3C). As for another case, third-generation (3G) mobile communication system patent portfolios will be set out in detail further on.

Patent pools are considered a highly efficient way to solve patent problems. But there is a risk that they could function as a tool for anticompetitive coordination or exclusion to restrict competition. While patent pools generally have some anti-competitive risk, the fact that they cover standards reinforces the risk. Competition laws (or antimonopoly law in Japan) have to regulate pools without overly blocking their efficient formation and utilisation.

There are patent pool cases regulated under antimonopoly law, some of which concern technical standards. Licensing practices have been a chief concern of the Fair Trade Commission of Japan (JFTC), which has issued guidelines, including one on patent pools. In the following sections, we look at possible effects and the regulations under the antimonopoly law in detail.

3 Standardisation, patent pools and competition: the Japanese case

The term 'patent pool' has been commonly used 'to convey the idea of a linking of the right to use patents issued to more than one patentee'.[11] The method of linking has varied; it can involve simple mutual agreement, concentration on one patent owner, or establishment of designated patent companies. Cross-licensed patents, which are not intended to license other parties, are also considered as constituting a pool.[12] Though the focus in the context of standardisation is on fairly large pools amassing a number of patents and establishing 'one-stop shopping', the form and size can still vary depending on the nature of standards and participants' willingness to cooperate. Below, I raise several pro-competitive effects that patent pools have, especially mega-pools with an accompanying one-stop patent clearing function. Though small pools may have more or less the same effect, it must be noted that the degree is not the same depending on its scale and size.

3.1 Pro-competitive effects[13]

(a) *Litigation cost*: Patent pools can reduce the cost and time for licensing and litigation, promote implementation of standards and accordingly bring about or activate competition. The effect is important especially for entrants who can hardly bear such costs and risk.

(b) *The complementary monopolies*: The amount of a licence fee can be reduced under patent pools compared with the case where each patent holder sets his own licence fee. In general, when several goods used complementarily are controlled by several different firms that have market power in their own controlling goods, the aggregated cost paid to these complementary goods by each buyer can be higher, and the total revenue that firms can accrue is less than when these are controlled by one firm. Complementary goods are in such a relationship that the price increase of one of them reduces the demand for others. When one firm controls all of them, the firm sets the price considering this effect, whereas when different firms have control, each firm sets its own profit-maximising price on each item without considering the demand-reducing effect on others' goods. The resulting price when several firms independently aim for profit maximisation is too high for aggregated profit maximisation. As for patents used complementarily, the effect is also true. The aggregated cost that the licensee has to pay could be higher when several patent owners with market power set their own royalty independently than when the price is set collectively by coordination among licensors, or by an organisation given the authority to sub-license. Patent pools resulting from such arrangements can reduce the cost for the licensee and at the same time increase total revenue for patentees. The cost cut promotes easier implementation of standards, and therefore competition, without reducing incentive for innovation.[14]

(c) *The lock-in effect*: A patent pool can reduce the risk of patent owners' opportunistic behaviour after implementation. The potential licensee is at risk of being abused by increases in royalty rate, demands of grant-back license without sufficient payment, and so on. Fear may cause under-investment of licensees, that is fewer licenses, less implementation, and less effort for further development. Patent pools can mitigate this when they provide more reliable commitment mechanisms compared with individual licences. Commitment is more likely when pools openly set the terms in advance for the attention of those who have good knowledge about the state of technology and the market (which we cannot always expect when the court solves licensing matters), and make an effort to keep a good reputation as a dedicated licensing organisation, which individuals might forego when they come near to exiting the market or when they compete in the implemented goods market with licensees.

(d) *Valuing*: Yet another expected function concerns assessing the value of patents. It is difficult to assess the value of patents, generally. It is even more difficult when the inventions covered are basically remote from commercialisation. Different industry backgrounds may alter the assessment – not only of the result, but also of the methods – which can make agreement impossible. It is the knowledge of the invention's potential, cost of implementation, the plan of commercialisation or successive development, that all help assessment. But such necessary knowledge is often shared among potential licensees and licensors, and communication among them is often difficult because it risks misappropriation. It is the failure of valuing, or the prospect of it, that blocks implementation accompanied by the fear of unacceptable royalty rates after implementation. Here also, well-designed patent pools can work. It may mitigate the problem to provide a high reliability of assessment by specialised institutes to assess and license, or to function as an independent neutral mediator which would not compete either with patentees or licensees.[15]

(e) *The need for pools in the context of standardisation and the state of competition in Japan*: While these efficiencies are found in patent pools in general, they are more obvious in the context of standardisation as analysed above. Generally, the effects are stronger where licensing is unavoidable (see effect (a)); the number of necessary licences is greater (effects (a) and (b)); patentees and potential licensees are competitors, which increases the risk of blocking and misappropriation (effects (a), (c) and (d)); the development of the market is uncertain, especially because getting a licence and settlement on terms is necessary before development (effects (c) and (d)); patentees are in frequent contact with potential licensees, which increases the risk of opportunistic behaviour (effect (c)); and the character of the relevant parties varies in the field of business, jurisdiction and, accordingly, patent enforcement practice, which makes it difficult to reach agreement on values (effect (d)). These conditions are, indeed, a description of the growing trend of standardisation.[16]

Further enhancing factors are found in the licensing practices emerging in Japan. So far, Japanese patent owners, especially in the field of electronics/ electric or machine manufacturers, who are some of the main actors in standardisation, have been limited in number and are relatively similar in size. They preferred a multi-product strategy, adopted similar technologies[17] and have had frequent contact in the product market as well as in licence negotiations. One study showed that major companies have formed close networks of licensing,[18] which might have been functioning as a promoter of their joint profit. But such conditions are changing against the background of globalisation and also big changes in patent practices.

After the phase of catching-up and losing advantage in the manufacturing industry, Japan is attempting a transition to a 'knowledge-based economy'. The reform of the patent system is the measure of primary importance for it. Patent law has been amended to realise stronger patent rights that can be enforced more quickly and easily.[19] Industry is, indeed, becoming interested more in patents and changing practices, which include a growing number of foreign applications.[20] Another implemented policy is the promotion of patent applications by universities and start-ups from them,[21] which significantly increase the number and variety of potential licensors/licensees who contact each other less frequently.[22] And, as in other jurisdictions, patents are expanding into new fields, especially with medical and business method patents. The utility of patent pools seems to be outright in these emerging conditions along with the traditional defects of the Japanese legal system such as the lengthy time for getting court decisions and a shortage of legal attorneys.

3.2 Anti-competitive effects

Patent pools can be anti-competitive, however. Anti-competitive effects can be caused in the following ways.[23]

(a) *Avoidance of competition between patents*: Patent owners compete when there are several patented technologies to achieve the same aim. Such competition can drag down the level of royalties. The straight way of avoiding such competition is to set a high royalty by agreement. Another is to collect competing patents into one licensing organisation. Such licensing organisations would set the price at the joint profit maximisation level. This is, indeed, a patent pool arrangement accompanied by a concentration of licence function. The concentration is the most straightforward when the licensing authority exclusively belongs to the organisation. Without such exclusivity, however, more subtle anti-competitive effects may emerge backed by coordination through intimate communication at patent pools, or a practical inability to get individual licences.

The result is, indeed, to create, maintain or strengthen market power which emerges through avoidance of competition among patents or technologies and can further distort competition in other markets through impeding active competition among goods, services or technologies, where patents in a market under the first market's power are input for the business.

(b) *Foreclosure*: Patent pools that collect patents necessary to provide goods or services, or conduct R&D, can eliminate others' competitive activities by refusing to grant a licence. Setting unfavourable terms can also impede vigorous competition. Such exclusion distorts competition and may result in market power depending on the status of excluded businesses and competition in the relevant markets. There are several ways to cause such exclusions, just as mergers between firms cause exclusion in many ways. The most prominent case would be that of competing patent owners collecting their patents, which are essential to conduct business, into a pool and excluding their competitors by refusing access to the patents. Access to collected complementary patents may be essential and may cause exclusion.

(c) *Keeping dubious patents intact*: The existence of a patent might impede others' competitive conduct. There is no doubt that setting a royalty patent increases the cost of licences, and therefore lessens competition compared with the status without the patent. Even when patentees do not demand royalties, the mere existence of the patent can inhibit competitors because of the risk. The existence of a patent, enforcing and requiring loyalty, is principally legitimate conduct under patent law. But this principle does not apply to the case where the right was maintained by unfair conduct. To maintain, or create the condition to maintain patents which otherwise would be determined invalid through trial, and restrain competition, constitutes anti-competitive conduct.

The most straightforward way to maintain dubious patents intact is to agree with each other and require the licensee not to contest the validity and coverage. A more subtle approach that might work would be just to license and reduce the incentive to contest. The entry deterrent effect is most likely when the patent is unavoidable but disputing validity is still costly and risky. It is often true that it is difficult for entrants to bear the cost and only able petitioners are incumbents with competing technologies. With the intention of blocking entrants, they might reach an agreement. They can share the anti-competitive profit by manipulating the scheme of royalties and sharing. In this case, they are maintaining their position through an arrangement that encourages keeping invalid patents that would otherwise disappear.

(d) *Restrictions of licensee's competitive behaviour*: Ancillary licence terms can restrict competition. The restriction on patents eliminates competition on price among licensees and vigorousness of competition in the market when the restriction covers enough of the industry. Other restrictions, such as on output, area, accompanying services and R&D efforts, may lessen the competition more than the effect inherent in the activities of licensing and obtaining royalty. The conditions such as exclusive use of licensed technologies, tying, boycotting the specified products and so on may cause exclusions and lessen competition. For patent pools that have enough power to set such terms, with wide coverage of the market and enforcement mechanisms, practising such schemes is easier.

(e) *State of competition in Japan and anti-competitive risk*: The risk of strategic use of pooling arrangements to avoid competition needs to be evaluated in view of recent trends in antimonopoly law enforcement. There are more straightforward strategies to avoid competition. Agreement among competitors to set product prices at a coordinated level is the simplest way to avoid competition. But such practices are getting more and more difficult under the stronger enforcement of antimonopoly law, which is represented by criminal sanctions against price-setting cartels.[24] Main participants in patent licensing and standardisation are still competitors in technologies and product markets. Patent pooling and/or using ancillary restraints can be more subtle alternatives.

Another danger is that patent pools function as a tool of exclusion. There is a notable patent pool case regulated under US anti-trust law as cheap Japanese products were excluded.[25] Now, facing a flood of imports from Asian countries, we have to be concerned that Japanese manufacturers may abuse patent pools to stop such competitive products.

The risk of exclusion against new start-ups is also worth close attention. Immaturity of financial markets, especially the scarcity of private risk capital, has been an obstacle for R&D efforts by smaller entrants.[26] The lack of experienced venture capitalists may provide a background for entry deterrent strategies based on patent rights.

4 Cases under antimonopoly law

The above analysis clearly demonstrates the need to establish functional regulation schemes for patent pools for promoting technical standards, which deter anti-competitive patent pool arrangements without inhibiting the pro-competitive use of it. How can and should the antimonopoly law meet the need?

The antimonopoly law regulates several aspects of patent pools. While it sets out that its provisions shall not apply to such acts recognisable as the exercise of rights under the Patent Act (Art. 21), it does not mean that every conduct relating to patents is exempted. The provision does not preclude application to arrangements not recognised as exercises, and agreements to pool licences and refuse the licence do not constitute such exercises. Furthermore, exercises are prohibited under antimonopoly law when, based on purpose, circumstances and the effect of conduct, it is considered an improper exercise not justified under patent law.[27] There is no dispute about the applicability of antimonopoly law to patent pooling; policy setting and conduct are regulated under antimonopoly law.[28]

Formation of a pool is prohibited under Art. 3, which prohibits entrepreneurs from restraining competition substantially in any particular field of trade, which is interpreted as creating, maintaining or strengthening market power in any relevant market, either by exclusion ('private monopolisation') or mutually restricting their business activities by contract, agreement or any other concerted actions with other entrepreneurs ('unreasonable restraint of trade'). When a pool is established as a new firm, a patent managing firm for example, whose interests are owned by, say, patent owners, it is scrutinised under Art. 10 (Prohibition of Particular Stockholding by a Company). The provision is part of Chapter 4 (Stock-holdings, Interlocking Directorates, Mergers, Divisions and Acquisitions of Business) and prohibits a firm from holding interest when it 'may have an effect to' restrain competition substantially. Under Art. 8, the business association is prohibited from restricting competition, limiting the present or future number of entrepreneurs and restricting the functions or activities of the constituent entrepreneurs unjustly. The latter two conducts are found under less strict standards compared with the substantial restraint of competition, and its activity relating to patent pools is regulated by the same token.

Aside from the above, individual conduct during the course of operation – such as coordination among competitors, refusal of licences, discriminatory treatment and restricting competitive activities through licence terms – is regulated under Art. 3, again as a 'private monopoly' or 'unreasonable restraint of trade' if it restricts competition substantially. As for the conduct of a business association, Art. 8 may be applied. In addition to these regulations, the practice mainly of potential trading partners, potential licensees in this context, is regulated under Art. 19, which prohibits designated 'unfair trade practices'. Designated unfair trade practices include unjust refusal to trade, discriminatory treatment, dealing on exclusive or restrictive terms and tying (Designation of Unfair Trade Practices (18 June 1982) Fair Trade Commission Notification No. 15). Unjustness here means a tendency to impede fair conditions. Such a tendency is found *inter alia* when it has a tendency to create market power by exclusion or restricting others' competitive activities.[29]

Antimonopoly law has infrequently, but occasionally, regulated patent pools up to now.[30] Some cases involved technical standards. The JFTC has set the guidelines on patent licence practices, which include the guidelines on patent pools. The following is a summary of the state of regulations on patent pools in general.

4.1 Licence guidelines

The JFTC licence guidelines,[31] which describe the JFTC view on the method and scope of applying the Antimonopoly Act to patents or know-how licensing agreements, state that patent pools, in general, can have a pro-competitive effect in terms of increasing the utility value of the said patents and so forth. However, promoting technological exchange among right holders, and thus, in themselves, do not pose a problem of unreasonable restraint of trade, there are cases when they have anti-competitive effects and need to be regulated. They show some examples of anti-competitive cases such as the following:

(a) The licensing agreements for the patents etc. are pooled in a corporate entity or organisation with the understanding of the members of the patent pool that they have accepted common restrictions, and the agreement imposes mutual restrictions on the members regarding the sale price, manufacturing volume, sales volume, sales outlets, sales territories etc. of the patented products etc. and substantially restricts competition in a market for particular products.

(b) Mutual restrictions may be imposed on the members of the patent pool regarding the fields of research and development, the parties to whom the licence may be granted or the technology that may be used, etc., thus substantially restricting competition in a market for particular products or particular technologies.

(c) Licences may be refused without justifiable reason, or other measures taken that have the effect of impeding the entry of other firms or of making it difficult for existing firms to conduct business. It may become difficult to conduct business activities in a particular field of trade without first obtaining licences for the patents, etc. of particular products because right holders competing in a market for the said products form a patent pool relevant to that particular field of trade and, consequently, agree to pool all existing and future improved technologies in the said patent pool.

As for the individual licence terms, the guidelines set detailed guidance for each kind of conduct such as restriction regarding scope of licence (duration, territory, technology), restrictions and obligations accompanying licensing (royalties, package licence, obligations regarding improved inventions, obligations not to contest the validity of the patent obligations etc.) and restrictions and obligations regarding manufacture of patented products (restrictions on prices, volume etc.). They are also applied to licensing activities concerning patent pools.

4.2 Cases

(a) Pharmaceutical case

The foreign patent owner Cesifu granted Fujisawa Yakuhin Kogyo (Pharmaceutical) K. K. the exclusive licence to manufacture and sale, which claimed its right against three other manufacturers, alleging they were infringing its right. They settled the dispute with an agreement that Fujisawa should not oppose the three companies' manufacturing and sales using their own developed method. In return, the three companies agreed, *inter alia*:

- that they should pay Fujisawa 7 per cent of sales as a 'consideration';
- that they should not contest the status of Fujisawa and Cesifu's patent;
- that all patent applications of the three companies should be shared with Fujisawa or Cesifu; and
- that they would cooperate to block others entering into the market.

Three companies also agreed to cooperate to stabilise the market with Fujisawa, and their price and output were restricted. Under their cooperation, new entrants were, indeed, alleged to have infringed the Fujisawa or Cesifu patents and terminated manufacturing and sales. As JFTC found these facts when the agreement period was near its end, it merely issued a warning and did not initiate a formal proceeding.[32]

(b) Pachinko case

A patent managing company, Nihon Yuugiki Tokkyo Unei Renmei (Nittokuren) (Japan Amusement Machine Patent Managing Federation), managed the patents and utility models covering pinball machines, 'Pachinko'. Since 1961, Nittokuren has operated a licensing business under rights granted by Pachinko machine manufacturers and patents that it acquired on its own. A law controlling amusement businesses, Huuzoku Eigyo Ho, sets the standards for the Pachinko machines and requires approval for their sale. It was difficult to get approval without the licensing of these patents. The pool was organised by members of a business association, Nihon Yuugiki Kougyou Kumiai (Nikkouso) (Japan Amusement Machine Manufacturer Association) and, among them, ten manufacturers, nine of which held important patents, held over 50 per cent of the interest directly or indirectly and sent personnel to the company as directors. The members of the Nikkouso, 19 manufacturers of Pachinko machines, took most of the share in the Pachinko machine market, and all of them were granted the licence from Nittokuren. In the licence terms, Nittokuren restricted cutting price and output. Nikkouso demanded and monitored its observation. When the entrants started threatening the positions in the Pachinko machine market, Nittokuren and ten major members set the policy to exclude entrants and refused the licence against new entrants. The termination clause was set when the licensee changed its operation status. This conduct inhibited new entrance, especially by the manufacture of a similar but different amusement machine, Pachinko Slot Machine.

In 1994, the JFTC found that Nittokuren and ten manufacturers were in violation of Art. 3, the prohibition of private monopoly through such conduct under the policy of eliminating new entrance, and issued a cease and desist order ('Elimination Measures'). It ordered ten companies and Nittokuren to void the policy, measures adopted under the policy relating to licensing, which was indeed the refusal of licence, and the termination clause in case of change of operation status. At the same time the JFTC issued a warning against them to refrain from restrictive conduct such as limiting price cuts, which are against Art. 3 and Art. 19. The JFTC also issued a warning under Art. 8 (1) against Nikkouso asking them to refrain from committing to the exclusion scheme and restricting cutting prices.

(c) Pachinko slot machine case

The Pachinko slot machine was an improved model of a slot machine introduced to Pachinko amusement halls during the 1980s under the abovementioned law regulating amusement services, 'Huuzoku Eigyou Ho'. Its manufacturers have been different from Pachinko machine manufacturers and they arranged their own pool. The machines are covered by many patents, and for manufacturers, settling the patent disputes was urgent. They established three different patent managing companies, which led the battle. Then, in 1993, a patent managing company, Nihon Dendousiki Yuugiki Tokkyo Kabusiki Kaisya (Japan Electric Amusement Machine Patent Co.) was established, for the purpose of unifying the management. Twenty-one companies established the company through equal investment, all of which were members of the association of the manufacturers, Nihon Dendousiki Yuugiki Kougyou Kyoudou Kumiai (Nichidenkyou) (Japan Electric Amusement Machine Manufacture Association). The participants granted sub-licensing rights to the company, and the company sold the sub-licensees a certificate stamp to be attached to the machine at 2,000 yen, which was the amount of the royalty. The royalty was collected from manufacturers, including patent owners. Half of the collected royalties were to be divided between patent owners in accordance with the usage report submitted by the sub-licensee and the subsequent decision of the patent assessment committee, the members of which were manufacturers and patent owners. The participants included those who did not own patent rights. The company licensed only the members of Nichidenkyou, which meant most of the Pachinko Slot manufacturers, collectively controlling almost 100 per cent of the market. Thirteen new entrants asked for the licence until March 1997 and were refused.

ARZE KK, which has an interest in the company and granted a sub-licence to the company, had many patent rights and distributed a 509 yen fee per machine in 1998 under the arrangement. ARZE was still dissatisfied with the revenue, thinking it was too low in consideration of its contribution to the pool, and thought that it would not get satisfactory revenue as long as it was counted based on the sub-licensee's voluntary usage report. After a proposition of termination of the arrangement and the change to individual licences, it started to offer individual licences, and in 1997, it began exercising its patent right, alleging infringement against other participants. It also claimed that ARZE was not obligated to pay royalties to the patent managing companies. A series of disputes were brought to court. ARZE argued particularly that the patent pool was against the anti-monopoly law, that the pooling arrangement was terminated and sub-licensing rights had expired, and that the patents alleged to be infringed were not included explicitly in the list of sub-licensed patents under the arrangement.

While the court found infringement of unlisted patents and ordered billions of yen damages, amounting to tens or millions of USD,[33] which was the largest damage amount at that time, the claim for the termination of the pool was denied. The court said that it was not apparent that the arrangement was against the antimonopoly law; noting that there was no evidence that participants refused licences under the policy to eliminate new entrance, restrained the outputs, were granted sub-license rights exclusively with the condition that the owners did not license by themselves, and aggregated essential patents into the company.[34]

(d) 3G case

Nineteen European, Korean and Japanese companies, which include electronics manufacturers and telecommunication service providers, produced a plan to set up a platform that would collect the essential patents covering standards of third-generation (3G) mobile communication systems. Several standards have been developed for 3G systems, including W-CDMA and CDMA-2000. They planned to set up a new patent framework characterised by greater flexibility in individual negotiations. Under the plan, patent owners and potential licensees were to conclude a framework agreement under which licensees could obtain licences whether under standard licence term or as an individually negotiated agreement. Under the standard licence, the standard royalty rate was set at 0.1 per cent per patent for the first phase, and maximum aggregate royalty to participants, 5 per cent per sales price, which applied to the agreement between each participant patent owner and licensees in a non-discriminatory manner. The licensee could obtain a licence from each individual patent owner by benefiting from a temporary licence under a preset term and dispute resolution measures in case of failure to reach agreement. Under the plan, participants would be obliged to submit all essential patents to the platform. Those who wanted to participate could do so. The scheme planned to set the evaluation panel, constituted with an independent organisation to collect only patents essential to implement any 3G standards. For management, an independent patent platform company was established.[35]

The plan was submitted to the Japan Fair Trade Commission for consultation (consultation on patent and know-how license),[36] and after analysis of its effects on competition (1) in the product market; (2) among technologies which utilise the same standards; and (3) among technologies which belong to different standards, the JFTC answered that it thought it would not take any action. The JFTC considered that, as long as the products' selling prices were not set and the information on those prices was not communicated among firms, the platform would not restrict competition in the product market either among products belonging to the same standards or ones belonging to different standards, based on several factors such as setting low and uniform aggregate rates and non-exclusiveness, in the sense that the platform would not prohibit individual agreements either to patent owners or to licensees.

As for competition among technologies 'within each standard', the plan was considered not to restrict competition because it collected only essential patents, not competitive ones. The JFTC devoted much space to an analysis of the competition among technologies which belonged to different standards. The conclusion was that there would be no problem because the competition among standards would not be active from the start. This was because incumbent telecommunication service providers would select a standard which planned to secure backward compatibility with second-generation (2G) systems like cdma2000 for cdmaOne, W-CDMA for GSM (the 2G standard used throughout Europe under the Directive), and equipment makers would follow the selection of telecom service providers. The competition among standards was considered to be most possible for new entrants into telecommunication services. But here also, the JFTC concluded that it was not serious because of room for individual negotiation. It thought the platform might even promote such competition because of the inclusion of all different standards.[37]

After the consultation, the US Department of Justice (DOJ) and the European Commission (EU) reviewed the plan, and significant changes were required during the course of these reviews.[38] Unlike JFTC, the DOJ considered that room for competition among standards was significant, particularly in view of the fact that many nations were awarding more licences for 3G services than they had for 2G, or making additional spectrum available which could be acquired by other operators. The most significant change was the separation of the licensing platform into five entities. Under the modified agreement, licensing was to be carried out by five platform companies, one for each of the five different standard technologies. They committed to making each platform have a separate licensing administrator and board of directors and set royalty rates independently. The licensing administrator was precluded from sharing competitively sensitive information. While they were allowed to have services from the same source, the services were restricted to those remote from setting licensing terms, such as patent evaluation services, education of third parties and industry-wide market research.[39]

4.3 Comment

The patent pool case relating to standardisation and giving an account of its nature is still rare. Nevertheless, these short descriptions demonstrate the ambiguous nature of the patent pool, the need for effective regulation and the work to be done towards this. Each pool has some benefits and bad effects. Various forms of pools can, indeed, restrict competition.

It seems that there has not been enough emphasis on the anti-competitive effect through avoidance of competition between patents, or their collections. It is too early to say that this is the trend in Japan, but at least the relationship between patents and/or licensing organisations has not been the reason for prohibition, and has been less emphasised in guidelines. The examples in the guidelines are about cases where obvious intent was found to cause anti-competitive effects in the product market or patented goods. In the Pachinko case, the JFTC ordered and warned simply against exclusive conduct through refusal of licences and restriction on price and output of patented goods, without mentioning anti-competitive risks caused from pooling itself. The absence of this was, indeed, a reason for the failure to convince the court of the anti-competitiveness of the Pachinko Slot patent pool.[40] Although in the US, too, it is not easy to find patent pools prohibited for the sole reason of competition avoidance among patents or maintenance of dubious patents intact, such concerns have been significant since early cases.[41]

The reason may be that interest has been focused on product markets, and it has been more effective for vertically integrated firms[42] to restrain competitive activities concerning products than ones concerning inputs (patents), where it is difficult to verify whether others are obeying the anti-competitive scheme. It may also be that it was difficult and time-consuming for competition authorities and courts to establish the relationship between patents and their effect on the changing technology market.

The regulated cases are undeniably typical ones which are necessary to keep regulated. But we should be concerned with other effects, too. The risk of such effects is rising with the increasing significance of the technology market. And in this area, too, more effort to disguise anti-competitive schemes would be taken as strengthening enforcement of the antimonopoly law. Even more probably, parties may conduct anti-competitive schemes surreptitiously. The court, too, may not notice the anti-competitive effect unless anti-competitiveness is apparent.

Improving the ability to evaluate patent pools is critical considering the irreversible nature of technologies. To put regulation into effect as well as not deterring the pooling arrangement unnecessarily, a patent pool should be better guided from its formation. We need a principle under which parties and the court are able to cope with less obvious anti-competitive effects taking into account the nature of standardisation.

It is not easy to set the principle. The diverse nature of patent pools and their significant potential to promote competition complicates the analysis and makes categorical analysis senseless. Generally, anti-competitive collusion is more likely where the firms in the market are limited in number, homogeneous and mature in technologies. The gap in technological ability was, indeed, a reason for the collapse of the Pachinko Slot Machine case. But this is not always the case. Patent pools make it easier to establish and enforce complicated coordination. The existence of solid business associations, which back the pool, increases the risk further. The Pachinko case exemplifies the danger.[43]

Patent pools are a type of joint sales arrangement. However, we cannot apply this reasoning here. The broad coverage, joint setting of the price, selling not only to customers but also to participants under the same term, and establishment of solid institutions that watch the observance of the sales term, are signs of anti-competitiveness of sales joint ventures (JVs). For the patent pools' technical standard, they might be inherent in the very nature of the pool for standard promotion and it is necessary to materialise its pro-competitive effect.

One of the typical anti-competitive pools has been considered with concentration of patents into one firm, which becomes dominant in the patented product market. When they can set the complicated mechanism sharing and divide the anti-competitive profit, such concentration is, indeed, better to maximise joint profits. In the US, such concentrations were created where the firm had already led the market before the concentration[44] and/or was in a better position to enforce patents to exclude competitors.[45] Needless to say, however, to create a single firm with a great deal of power in the product market should not be a necessary condition of regulation.

5 Review under antimonopoly law

5.1 Framework

There are several ways for patent pools to affect competition, as we have already seen. Though they do not constitute an exhaustive list, they are typical and the competition effect analysis can be performed in view of these typical ways. The plaintiff can establish how the patent pool restricts competition and the defendant can claim pro-competitive effects described above. There will always be some pro-competitive effects. Apparent anti-competitive effects should be justified only when the effect is sufficient to redeem any anti-competitive effect in the short term and when it is established with committed measures.

The factor to be considered differs depending on how the patent pool affects competition. However, in most cases, the position of the collected patents and the competition status in the relevant market, which are usually measured with market shares, would be relevant though not decisive. The market that should be considered may be one constituted with a series of technologies which are competing with each other to dominate the market as a standard; patents or technologies to implement one particular standard; products that interoperate with a series of other standardised products; or licensing organisations including individual patent owners.

When analysing the position of the patent, it is necessary to consider the importance and usefulness of the inventions covered. Here, the importance and usefulness need to be valued in economic terms, not in technical advancement terms, although these values can give some insight into the economic value of inventions. In this context, it is important to see the position of patents as a whole, as well as seeing the position of each patent.

The competition among goods should be considered separately, as vigorous competition between patents does not necessarily result in vigorous competition in the goods market. The possibility of coordination through disguised pooling arrangements, under which there are trivial patent licences with restricted competitive conduct has, indeed, been one of the biggest concerns for patent pools.[46]

In the case of patent pools for promoting technical standards, the position of the standard gives useful insight into the status of competition. Being a standard does not mean strong position. There are a number of standards set by quite minor firms that compete vigorously with other interchangeable goods.[47] Even when a standard occupies a dominant share, the competition between standardised products and non-standardised ones may be possible using converters. We should avoid hasty conclusions from the form or the alleged title of technology. However, when the law or an administrative regulation mandates the implementation, the strong position may be found quite easily.

Competition between licensing entities has relevance as it limits the power of pools. Where the patent pool does not yield a significant cost-cut, those who want a licence can simply go to other entities, either other managing companies or individual patent owners, to negotiate a better bargain. So far, this consideration has been reduced to the analysis of whether a patent pool takes the better position in terms of transaction cost or by a position as a sole licensing authority attained from patent owners. But where there is competition between patent management services, which is, indeed, emerging these days, the competition between licensing organisations is viewed differently.

In principle, a stronger position and/or broader coverage necessitates a more cautious approach in establishing, organising and setting the licensing policy of patent pools so that they do not cause anti-competitive effects. We can safely say that a patent pool with less than a 20 per cent share in any relevant market would not restrict competition as long as there are no extraordinary factors. On the other hand, for a pool with a stronger position, its organisation, policy and conduct should be reviewed under a stricter standard.

Seeing the effect of conduct in the conditions of these relevant markets, when conducts are considered to have both a pro- and anti-competitive effect, we have to balance the effects and determine whether it has the effect required by the relevant law.

Practically, however, such market analysis is very difficult in the new technology area, especially when it concerns competition among standards in the information and/or communication field, where a drastic transformation is possible because of the network effect, or the strong needs of interoperability or compatibility in the field where innovation is the driving force of the market. We cannot leave pools until anti-competitive effects are manifested, when regulation would mean little after the development of the market. But too much intervention should also be avoided as it also delays the development of competition.

The better approach would be to utilise a rule of thumb on conduct in consideration of the available economic data. It would be appropriate to require a patent pool that appears to have a strong position to take precautionary measures in terms of managing structure and licensing policy. Under such conditions, a pool should be cleared even if it would take a strong potential position. The rule which sets the standard for conduct categorically has been criticised for its lack of relevance to economic effect. In Japan, there is, indeed, a need to establish an improved economic method of analysis. But against this background, it should also be noted that economic analysis does not always deliver a promising result.

Several rules of thumb concerning licensing practices have been developed. In view of the nature and alleged object of patent pools, we can set out some presumptions, such as that patent pools without measures preventing anti-competitive patents licence practices should be considered anti-competitive. The recent US cases[48] and summaries of them[49] are useful and noted by many antimonopoly law scholars in Japan.[50]

The following is a summary of such rules of thumb which takes account of regulation practice in several jurisdictions, especially in the US, where several patent pools have been reviewed under its competition law – Antitrust Law – which the writer considers appropriate under antimonopoly law in Japan. It is not exhaustive and there are unresolved matters, as we shall see. So they are, rather, provisional points to consider which are highly relevant for any patent pools and which would assist the analysis. For the purposes of simplification, they are categorised into three groups: (a) the way to collect patents; (b) licensing policy; and (c) the relationship between patent owners. However, it must be noted that they are closely interrelated in the determination of legality. For example, when reviewing legality of formation, the licensing policy, the institutional setting and measures should be considered. They are concerned with the effect of pooling agreements to create pools and would help to know their aim.

5.2 Points for consideration

5.2.1 What to collect

The relationship between patents may be categorised as either (a) blocking; (b) complementary; or (c) competing or interchangeable. The patents are said to be blocking if practising one patent inevitably causes the infringement upon another patent. Patents are complementary when patented products' users need another patent licence to attain the intended or better results, though the licence is not necessary for practice. When there are several patents that cover inventions that enable equivalent results and can be used interchangeably, the patents are competing or interchangeable. It is when the collected patents are blocking or complementary that collecting patents into a pool promotes competition through cutting the cost of negotiation, reducing the fear of opportunistic behaviour, and reducing the sum of the licence fee. When the patents are competing, collecting them into pools does not cause these benevolent effects. Such pools are more likely to emerge or increase the power to raise the licence fee through restricting competition between patents and to eliminate rivals and/or to restrict competition in goods and services. The validity of the patent should be a precondition for blocking relationships or complementarities, as unenforceable patents should not block any usage in the end. As such, validity should have relevance in the determination of the anti- or pro-competitiveness of the pool. Pooling unenforceable patents also increases or maintains the barrier for entrance through decreasing the incentives to dispute the validity of collected patents.

(A) VALIDITY OF PATENTS

When a pool has a wide coverage of patents in the industry with a great number of licences, which in total have (or will have) a substantial share in the relevant market, each patent's validity should be confirmed before being organised into a pool. But the cost and time incurred between disputes delays implementation, and getting a secured position against infringement allegations has some benefit. Such benefits should be taken into consideration even if the rate of invalidation is not low, and the possibility of claims is the best accelerator of disputes. So for most cases, a patent grant should give a presumption for validity in antimonopoly cases.

(B) RELATIONSHIP BETWEEN PATENTS

The blocking and/or complementarities are a matter of degree because there can always be some way to proceed without the licence if less effective technologies or costly development are considered as alternatives. In principle, when the relevant market is less competitive, the higher standard is appropriate.

(C) THE INDEPENDENT REVIEW OF VALIDITY AND THE RELATIONSHIP
AMONG PATENTS

The review of validity and relationship by a person/organisation independent from pools, licensors and licensees is a good scheme to contain anti-competitive risks. Independence should mean the separation of entity, conclusiveness of their determination, secured position and a salary/fee that never relates to their determination.

(D) MAINTENANCE OF INCENTIVES FOR LICENSORS/LICENSEES TO
MONITOR

Securing the incentives for licensors/licensees to keep constituents of a pool competitive by way of disputing validity or the necessity of others' patents is necessary, especially when the pool covers most of the candidates who have incentives and capabilities to dispute in practice. Such incentives can be maintained through the licence fee and its distribution scheme based on the number of licensed patents. It is unnecessary to add that the absence of non-contest clauses is a precondition for the effort to keep a portfolio pro-competitive.

(E) IMPROVEMENT

The prohibition on grant-back clauses works to prevent the pool from growing to include competing patents and also from eliminating incentives of licensees to conduct R&D efforts. However, it is still efficient to include patents covering improvements that are necessary for the implementation of the standard. In the US cases, it has been permissible to require grant-back when it is blocking or complementary with the originally pooled patents with reasonable consideration.

5.2.2 The licensing policy

(A) REASONABLE AND NON-DISCRIMINATORY LICENSING

Pooling a large number of useful patents will create the power of restricting competition through excluding competitors. Here, exclusion means not only the complete blocking of entrance or withdrawal from the market, but also reducing the ability and incentives to compete actively. Such conduct generally contradicts the aim of pooling: promotion of standards. Easing the fear of being abused would facilitate promotion of effective licensing, on the other hand.

Reasonableness and non-discrimination are hard to determine in practice, however. Establishment of an independent dedicated licensing organisation that would not have a natural incentive to eliminate potential licensees anti-competitively and giving it authority to license might be the best measure for coping with the problem.

(B) PACKAGE LICENSING

Package licensing is a form of tying arrangement under which patents are licensed only as a whole. Tying sales are regulated under Art. 19 of the Antimonopoly Act when they are coerced and considered to have a tendency to impede fair competition. Such a tendency has been found in several ways, including an exclusionary effect in the market, invasion of the freedom of selection on the part of buyers, and improperness as a means of competition as the arrangement utilises the position of goods, rather than their merit. Coercion has been interpreted broadly to include economic coercion by use of economic power in the tying goods.

In the context of patent pools, too, coercion should be found unless the pooled patents do not have any power over negotiating and obtaining the licence from another source is practically possible. And to justify tying licences, there should be conditions such as the fact that packaging is necessary to make the arrangement practical by cutting administration costs, or that packaged patents are always used as a combination in practice.

(C) LIMITATION ON COMPETITIVE CONDUCT OF LICENSEES

It is generally unnecessary to set the price and output of patented goods, and it should be regulated unless justified. While licence with royalty always constrains the competitive activity as far as it increases the cost, setting royalty and setting price of the patented goods are not the same. Given the rate of royalty, there still is room for competing, for example, by cutting the cost. Price and output are highly sensitive competitive matters, while they rarely have the effect to promote standardisation and competition, and they should be decided independently. The restriction on less sensitive matters should be analysed in relation to its aim and effect.

5.2.3 Limitation on competitive conduct of patent owners

(A) COORDINATION IN THE GOODS/SERVICES MARKET AND EFFORTS IN R&D

The restricting or coordinating of competitive behaviour concerning goods uncovered by pooled patents is unnecessary in most cases. Coordination among competitors on price or output is highly anti-competitive and effective. Such conduct should be determined to be illegal without detailed analysis.

It should be noted that anti-competitive coordination is possible without explicit restriction. The exchange of information on competitive-sensitive matters should be prohibited. When competitors having substantial shares are concerned in the pool, setting a firewall should be a requirement.

(B) INDEPENDENCE OF THE LICENSING ORGANISATION

Here, too, the independence of the licensing organisation has meaning, because such an organisation has less incentive to promote coordination in other markets. It could also collect necessary information without causing anti-competitive information sharing.

(C) NON-EXCLUSIVE LICENSE TO POOL

This is the last guarantee that the licensee should not give the licensing organisation sole authorisation to license. Non-exclusivity is also critical for competing licensing organisations to emerge. Unless the exclusivity is considered to have no effect in view of competition among patent holders and among licensing entities, strong justification, such as the need to concentrate to attain the minimum viable scale, should be required.

6 Unresolved problems and concluding remarks

As discussed above, a patent pool has an excellent function that is able to maintain the amount of licence fee as an appropriate amount, prevailing technology and secure licence revenue. This function has an important meaning especially in the context of a pool that collects patents covering standards which, by nature, enhance the value of a patent. It is expected that this type of a patent pool is used from now on and affects the potential of a company to utilise a patent right. At the same time, however, a patent pool has an undesirable effect from a point of view of public interest and competition in particular. Japanese competition law – anti-monopoly law – sets limits for patent pools, their organisation and licensing practices. In this chapter, we have seen the current status of the regulations under antimonopoly law and considered directions that regulations should follow.

Overall analysis shows desirability of an independent licensing organisation, especially if the pool has a wide coverage of competitors and controls the essential patent. This chapter has also set out some market share standards and points for consideration. These might be of some help, however, as the competition effect may be significantly varied and economic analysis has a limitation, so that the efficacy of the regulation may depend on a case-by-case reasoning process. We have explained some typical anti-competitive and pro-competitive effects that patent pools may bring about, and which may be useful for the reasoning process.

There are several unresolved problems. Which patent should be pooled when the result S can be attained with a patent combination of either A + B + X, A + B + Y? Neither X nor Y should be pooled because they have alternatives? Then how about when X is highly necessary for a majority of it to be compatible with their installed technology? In this situation, considering economising the transaction cost, is the pool of A + B + X allowed? In such an arrangement, not only Y but also the consumer may suffer if Y has a potential to grow popular. Organising a separate pool, A + B + X and A + B + Y may be the solution, but it is not always possible and sometimes ineffective because they have a common element A + B. Rigid separation increases the establishment cost, which may make a second pool impossible. The problem involves the trade-off between competition and efficiency through the cutting of transaction costs. It is also a variation of the old problem concerning JV (joint venture) and a boycott, where access to JV may cause coordination while refusal of it may cause exclusion. This problem, indeed, causes a different conclusion. While the view of room for competition between different 3G standards may be the primary reason for the sharp contrast in the need to establish a separate licensing company, one may see a different emphasis between DOJ and JFTC. The trade-off concerning transaction costs is also manifest in the problem of treatment of non-essential, but relevant patents. Some parties hope to collect the relevant patents, or to include a grant-back clause on relevant patents. The legality of the conduct in the context of influential pools is still under discussion.

So far, and in the above analysis too, competition among licensing organisations is not focused. If it is, such competition would be beneficial. In the patent licensing area, the organisation is at its inception and the future of the competition is still uncertain.

One pro-competitive effect that has not been mentioned is that of promoting competition by creating strong market power which is otherwise deemed impossible, collecting more royalties and increasing the incentive to innovate. This has not been previously mentioned in this chapter, not because it *would* not happen, but because it *should* not happen, in my opinion. The problem involves our old, familiar and everlasting controversy about the relationship between industrial policy and anti-monopoly law.

In the above antimonopoly analysis, the transaction cost of individual negotiation and litigation cost, and the possibility for each technology holder to block standardisation are exogenous. For legal analysis of each patent pool under antimonopoly, these factors have to be given because each arrangement has only an insignificant effect on them. The patent pool is, rather, an answer given these factors. But for public policy, these other exogenous factors are not given. There might be other ways to reduce the transaction cost. The policy concerning university research, patent, management and so forth affects the cost. Encouraging training in licence law, highly technical areas and international negotiation will also be effective. The Japanese judicial system has tremendous room for improvement.[51] These issues should be considered particularly after knowing that a patent pool, which is aimed at reducing the burdens of each patent right holder as well as judicial system by easing licence negotiations and undertaking a value evaluation function, is not always beneficial.

Notes

1   This is the English version of 'Standardisation, Patent Pools and Antimonopoly Law' (Japanese) 49 Hogaku Zassi (*Osaka City University Law Journal*) 435–88 (2002), written in September 2002. The author made a considerable number of changes for English readers and revised/updated the text following the development of cases. For literature and documents in Japanese and detailed discussion concerning the interpretation of the Antimonopoly Act, please see the Japanese version.

2   Definitions of standard at public standardisation bodies and in laws are constrained by their mandates and/or their normative context. For example, International Organization for Standardization (ISO) set its definition as 'document, established by consensus and approved by a recognized body, that provides, for common and repeated use, rules, guidelines or characteristics for activities or their results, aimed at the achievement of the optimum degree of order in a given context'. *ISO/IEC Guide 2*: 1996, Standardization and related activities – General vocabulary 3.2. The author abstracted general features of standards so that the definition here should cover well enough what has been considered as a standard.

3   Based on their functions, standards are categorised into interoperability standards, compatibility standards and quality standards. *ISO/IEC Guide 2*: 1996, General vocabulary 2.2, 2.3 and 5.7.

4   For regulations on practices relating to standards under antimonopoly law, see JFTC, *Gizyutu hyozyun to kyoso seisaku ni kansuru kenkyukai hokokusyo* (Report of the Study Group on the Technical Standard and Competition Policy) (July 2000) available at http://www.jftc.go.jp/pressrelease/cyosa.htm (Japanese); Noriyuki Doi (ed.), *Gizyutu Hyozyun to Kyoso* (The Technical Standard and Competition) (Tokyo: Nippon-Hyoron-Sha Co. Ltd, 2001). As for standard setting activity by industry, the author published 'Standard Setting and Antimonopoly Law', 53 *Hokkaido Law Review* 1048 (2002) (Japanese). For detailed analysis of the regulation under Antitrust Law, see James J. Anton and Dennis A. Yao, 'Standard-Setting Consortia, Antitrust, and High-Technology Industries', 64 *Antitrust Law Journal* 247 (1995).

5   As for compulsory licensing, Japanese patent law sets so-called 'arbitration' procedures, under which the commissioner of the patent office can require a patent

owner to grant a licence when patent owners do not utilise the right sufficiently (Art. 83), another patent owner needs the licence (Art. 92), or when the working of a patented invention is 'particularly necessary in the public interest' (Art. 93). But they have never used this power. For its background and discussion, see 'Symposium, Compulsory License of Patent', 24 *Annual of Industrial Property Law* 93 (2000) (Japanese).

6 Standardisation bodies, especially public ones, have set their own 'patent policy' or 'IPR policy'. For that of the JISC, see JISC '*Tokkyoken wo fukumu JIS no seitei ni kansuru tetuduki ni tuite* (On establishment of JIS covered by patents)' (February 2001), available at http://www.jisc.go.jp/jis-act/proposal.html (Japanese); for ISO, see ISO/IEC Directives, Part 2, Rules for the structure and drafting of International Standards 2.14.1–3 and Annex H 1–3 (2001). The policy typically states that the standard body should collect information on the relevant patents, especially through requiring the disclosure of relevant patents when firms submit a draft of standards for consideration, try to avoid using technologies which are covered by a patent and, when inevitable, use such technologies only when the owner promises to license under reasonable and non-discriminatory terms. Policies vary on several points, such as the coverage for copyrights, the width of obligation of disclosure and the disadvantage to those who do not obey the obligation. See Mark A. Lemley, 'Intellectual Property Rights and Standard-Setting Organisations', 90 *California Law Review* 1889 (2002). Academics and the Japanese fair trade commission are arguing the possibility of applying anti-monopoly law to the unilateral refusal to license by a patent owner, but this has also never been applied so far in practice.

7 For the arrangement, its analysis and antitrust cases concerning the pool, see *Zenith Radio Corp. v. Radio Corp. of America*, 106 F. Supp. 561 (D. Del. 1952); Application of Radio Corp. of America, 13 F.R.D. 167 (SDNY 1952); *United States v. RCA*, 1958 Trade Cas. (CCH) P69, 164 (1958); *Zenith Radio Corp. v. Hazeltine Research*, 395 U.S. 100 (1969).

8 See MPEG-LA, http://www.mpegla.com/ (visited 31 May 2003). See also *United States Department of Justice Antitrust Division* (hereinafter *DOJ*) *Business Review* letter from Joel Klein to Gerrard R. Beeney, Esq. (26 June 1997) http://www.usdoj.gov/atr/public/busreview/1170.htm

9 See DVD6C Licensing Agency, http://www.dvd6cla.com/ (visited 31 May 2003). See also *DOJ Business Review* Letter from Joel I. Klein to Carey R. Ramos, Esq. (10 June 1999) http://www.usdoj.gov/atr/public/busreview/2485.htm

10 See *DOJ Business Review* Letter from Joel I. Klein, to Garrard R. Beeney, Esq. (16 December 1998) http://www.usdoj.gov/atr/public/busreview/2121.htm

11 *United States v. Line Material Co.*, 333 U.S. 287, 314 n. 24 (1948).

12 See, e.g., Joel I. Klein, Cross Licensing and Antitrust Law n. 3, Address Before the American Intellectual Property Law Association (2 May 1997), available at http://www.usdoj.gov/atr/public/speeches/1123.htm. According to the US Antitrust Scholar Hovenkamp, the term 'pool' is 'nothing more than an arrangement under which two or more firms share some input, usually with some agreed-upon formula for dividing expenses' and 'The metaphor of the pool is taken from the oil industry, where multiple surface owners might have an interest in the same subterranean pool of oil'. XII Herbert Hovenkamp, *Antitrust Law* 232 (New York: Aspen Publishing, 1999). There have, indeed, been many cases of restricting competition by jointly controlling or sharing inputs in general, final products, revenue or interest as well as patents. See, e.g., *Addyston Pipe & Steel Co. v. United States*, 175 U.S. 211 (1899); *United States v. Corn Products Refining Co.*, 234 F. 964 (1916). Some states' antitrust laws prohibit anti-competitive pools as well as agreement or trust. See, e.g. Code of Ala. §8–10–1 (2002); C.R.S. 6–4–121 (2001); HRS §480–4 (2001). For its historical importance, see William

Z. Ripley, 'Introduction', in *Trusts, Pools and Corporations* xiii (revised edn, Boston: Ginn & Co., 1916).

13 The competition effect is summarised in Sadao Nagaoka, *Gizyutu hyozyun he no kigyokan kyoryoku* (Cooperation among firms toward technical standards), 35 *Sosiki Kagaku* 39–41 (2001). For the detail, see literature cited in the following notes.

14 Carl Shapiro, 'Setting Compatibility Standards: Cooperation or Collusion?' in Rochelle Cooper Dreyfuss, Diane Leenheer Zimmerman and Harry First (eds), *Expanding the Boundaries of Intellectual Property: Innovation Policy for the Knowledge Society* 94 (New York: Oxford University Press, 2001); Carl Shapiro, 'Navigating the Patent Thicket: Cross Licenses', in Adam B. Jeffe, Josh Lerner and Scott Stern (eds), *Innovation Policy and the Economy* (Cambridge, MA: MIT Press, 2001).

15 Robert P. Merges, 'Institutions for Intellectual Property Transactions: the Case of Patent Pools', in Rochelle Cooper Dreyfuss, Diane Leenheer Zimmerman and Harry First (eds), *Expanding the Boundaries of Intellectual Property: Innovation Policy for the Knowledge Society* (New York: Oxford University Press, 2001).

16 Shiro Takeda, Masaki Kaziura and Yasuro Uchida, *Kokusai Hyozyun to Senryaku Teikei* (International Standards and Strategic Alliances) (Tokyo: Chuokeizai-Sha, Inc., 2001).

17 Shigeru Asaba, *Nihon Kigyo no Kyoso Genri* (Toyo Keizai Inc., 2002).

18 *Hajime Yamada, Gizyutu Kyoso to Sekai Hyozyun* (Technology Competition and Global Standard) 115–16 (Tokyo: NTT Publishing Co. Ltd. 1999).

19 See Toshiko Takenaka, 'International and Comparative Law Issues: Patent Infringement Damages in Japan and the United States: Will Increased Patent Infringement Damage Awards Revive the Japanese Economy?' 2 *Washington University Journal of Law and Policy* 309 (2000).

20 See Japan Patent Office, 'Trends of Industrial Property Right Applications and Registrations' (22.10.2002), available at http://www.jpo.go.jp/shiryou_e/index.htm. The DVD6C pools are keen about enforcement in China. See DVD6C Licensing Agency, News, http://www.dvd6cla.com/news.html (visited 31 May 2003). The journal of Japan Intellectual Property Association, *Chizai Kanri* (Intellectual Property Management), is constantly reporting Japanese Firms' IPR policy in Japanese. In English, see, e.g., Takashi Nakayama, 'Increase and Change in IPR at the Toshiba Corporation', in Ruth Taplin (ed.), *Exploiting Patent Rights and a New Climate for Innovation in Japan* (London: Intellectual Property Institute, 2003).

21 Several articles in Ruth Taplin (ed.), *Exploiting Patent Rights and a New Climate for Innovation in Japan* (London: Intellectual Property Institute, 2003) are exploring the recent trend, background and cases.

22 As for the additional factors inhibiting efficient licensing concerning patents held by researchers at universities, see Michael A. Heller and Rebecca S. Eisenberg, 'Can Patents Deter Innovation? The Anti-commons in Biomedical Research', 280 *Science* 698 (1998).

23 See Roger B. Andewert, 'Analysis of Patent Pools under the Antitrust Laws', *Antitrust Law Journal* 53: 611, 617–19 and 628–9 (1984); John H. Barton, 'Antitrust Treatment of Oligopolies with Mutually Blocking Patent Portfolios', 69 *Antitrust Law Journal* 851, 865–6 and 876–7 (2001).

24 JFTC, Annual Report on Competition Policy is available at http://www.jftc.go.jp/e-page/report/annual/index.html. Kenji Sanekata and Stephan Wilks, 'The Fair Trade Commission and the Enforcement of Competition Policy in Japan', in G. Bruce Doern and Stephan Wilks (eds), *Comparative Competition Policy* 102 (1996) provides historical and political overview as well as the 'renaissance' in the early 1990s. Further strengthening is considered necessary. As for overall

status of the enforcement regime and change, see James D. Fry, 'Struggling to Teethe: Japan's Antitrust Enforcement Regime', *The Journal of Law and Policy in International Business* 32: 825 (2001).

25 *United States v. Singer Mfg. Co.*, 374 U.S. 174 (1963).

26 See Yutaka Imai and Masaaki Kawagoe, 'Business Start-ups in Japan: Problems and Policies', *Oxford Review of Economic Policy* 16(2): 114 (2000).

27 See JFTC, 'Guidelines for Patent and Know-how Licensing Agreements Under the Antimonopoly Act Part 2' (30 July, 1999), available at http://www.jftc.go.jp/e-page/guideli/patent99.htm

28 Akira Negishi, 'Patent Pools' (Japanese), in *Hanrei License Ho* (The License Law: Case Analysis) (Hatumei Kyokai (Japan Institute of Invention and Innovation), 2000).

29 Mitsuo Matsushita, 'The Antimonopoly Law of Japan', in Edward M. Graham and J. David Richardson (eds), *Global Competition Policy* 151 (1997) is the recent concise description of the antimonopoly law, written in English.

30 *Toshihumi Hienuki, Titekizaisanken to Dokusen Kinshi Ho* (Intellectual Property and Antimonopoly Law) §2–2–2 (Yuhikaku Publishing Co., Ltd, 1994) detailed cases and their legal appraisals.

31 JFTC, 'Guidelines for Patent and Know-how Licensing Agreements under the Antimonopoly Act' (30 July 1999), available at http://www.jftc.go.jp/e-page/guideli/patent99.htm. For informative detailed comparative analysis based on a good explanation of its background, development and contents, see Joshua A. Newberg, 'Technology Licensing under Japanese Antitrust Law', 32 *The Journal of Law and Policy in International Business* 705 (2001).

32 A warning against Fujisawa Yakuhin Kogyo K.K., 23 April 1982.

33 Decision of the Tokyo High Court, 16 July 2001; Decision of the Tokyo District Court, 31 October 2000 and 19 March 2002, 25 June 2002.

34 Decision of the Tokyo High Court, 19 March 2002 (7.4 billion yen (62 million USD) damage ordered). Against another defendant, 0.9 billion yen (7.5 million USD) damage was ordered on the same day. Decision of the Tokyo High Court, 19 March 2002.

35 About the original plan, see Hisashi Kato, '*Daisansedai idotai tusin no tame*' (no patent platform licence) (for 3G mobile communication), 51 *Chizai Kanri* 559 (2001).

36 Information on Prior Consultation System, or '*Jizen Soudan Seido*', is available at http://www.jftc.go.jp/jizen/index.htm (regrettably, Japanese only).

37 JFTC, 'Press Release on Prior Consultation Regarding Establishment of 3G Patent Platform' (Japanese), 14 December 2000, available at http://www.jftc.go.jp/press-release/00.december/00121402.htm

38 See DOJ Press Release (12 November 2002) http://www.usdoj.gov/atr/public/press_releases/2002/200454.htm and European Commission, Press Release IP/02/1651 (12 November 2002) available at http://europa.eu.int/rapid/start/cgi/guesten.ksh

39 *DOJ Business Review* letter from Charles A. James to Ky P. Ewing, Esq. (12 November 2002) http://www.usdoj.gov/atr/public/busreview/200455.htm. Under the plan, the portfolio companies were not to offer a package licence. Instead, they set default standards and interim licences and dispute resolution procedures. The reason for not offering one-stop shopping was the desire of the parties to attract broader potential licensors. The arrangement was seen favourably by the DOJ as it prevented the patent owners, who also had a significant interest as licensees, from abusing the collective power through a platform company against other patent owners whose interest is as licensors.

40 Another collusion case also involves apparent anti-competitive collusion in the patented products market. See JFTC, Recommendation Decision, 5 May 1970,

17 *Shinketsushu* 86. In the case, six concrete pile manufacturers holding patents jointly set the share of output and agreed that they should license their own patents to firms on condition that the licensee should also obey the agreed output restriction. They also agreed to get permission before they could license their own patents. The JFTC found that they were against the prohibition of the restraint of trade under Art. 3 by restricting competition in the sales of pile and issued a cease and desist order.

41 *Standard Oil Co. v. United States*, 283 U.S. 163, 174–5 (1931). As for the maintenance of invalid patents, see *United States v. Singer Mfg. Co.*, 374 U.S. 174, 190 (1963).

42 Goto Akira, 'Japan's National Innovation System: Current Status and Problems', *Oxford Review of Economic Policy* 16(2): 103 (2000) presents a brief and to the point explanation of Japanese corporate structure in point of innovation.

43 In the US, see, e.g., *United States v. United States Gypsum Co.*, 333 U.S. 364 (1974). It is suggested that the arrangement in the Medicine case might have functioned as a 'ceasefire deal' where the launch of new medicine is usually followed by competitive development of similar medicine. Toru Nakamura, Case note, 381 *Kosei Torihiki* 27, 30 (1982).

44 See, e.g., *Kobe, Inc. v. Dempsey Pump Co.*, 198 F.2d 416 (10th Cir.), cert. denied, 344 U.S. 837 (1952).

45 See, e.g., *United States v. Singer Mfg. Co.*, 374 U.S. 174 (1963).

46 See, e.g., *United States v. New Wrinkle, Inc.*, 342 U.S. 371, 374 (1952).

47 Case No. IV/M.2439 Hitachi/STMicroelectronics/SuperH JV(OJ C252, 12.09. 2001, p. 22) is an illustrative case though it involved not only licensing but also development. In this case, two microelectronics manufacturers, Hitachi Ltd and STMicroelectronics N.V. planned to establish a new JV, SuperH, to whom they planned to transfer IP and its authority to license relating microprocessor architecture, SuperH4. The parent company planned to continue to be active in its neighbouring downstream and downstream market, and Hitachi was to conduct license business concerning SH1–3 architectures. The EC Commission decided not to oppose based on, *inter alia*, the low share (0–15%) of architecture and partners microprocessors.

48 See the *Business Review* letter cited in notes 7–9. Also suggestive are several antitrust cases concerning Radio Corporation of America. See the case cited in note 6.

49 The US Patent and Trademark Office White Paper on Patent Pools: A Solution to the Problem of Access in Biotechnology Patents (January 2001), available at http://www.uspto.gov/web/offices/pac/dapp/opla/patpoolcover.html

50 Noboru Kawahama, '*Gizyutu Hyozyun to Dokusen Kinsi Ho*' (The Technical Standard and Antimonopoly Law), *Hogakuronso* (Kyoto Law Review) 146: 129–31 (2000), Akira Negishi, 'Antitrust and Patent Pool' (Japanese), in *Titeki Zaisan Ho no Keihu* 818–19 (Tokyo: Seirinshoin, 2002); Toshihumi Hienuki, '*Joho syakai to kyoso seisaku*' (Information Society and Competition Policy) *Horitsu Jiho* 73: 37–8 (2001).

51 As for the need to strengthen handling of cases requiring specialised knowledge recognised in the fundamental judicial reform undertaken now in Japan, see, The Justice System Reform Council, Recommendations of the Justice System Reform Council (12 June 2001), available at http://www.kantei.go.jp/foreign/policy/ sihou/singikai/990612_e.html. Several reforms are under consultation at Consultation Group on Intellectual Property Litigation, http://www.kantei.go.jp/ jp/singi/sihou/kentoukai/11titeki.html (Japanese). For an overview from a broader perspective, see Kahei Rokumoto, 'Law and Culture in Transition', 49 *American Journal of Comparative Law* 545 (2001) (Japanese Law Symposium).

8 Redefining brand valuation within the Japanese context

Akito Tani

Introduction

In accordance with the structural changes in the economic environment caused by the so-called 'new economy', advances in IT development and deregulation have resulted in corporations being confronted with a paradigm shift from a 'tangible business strategy', based on tangible business resources including financial assets, property and equipment, land, etc. (referred to as 'tangibles' hereafter), to an 'intangible business strategy', based on intangible business resources including intellectual property, research and development, and business know-how (referred to as 'intangibles' hereafter).

When implementing an 'intangible business strategy', it is important to further enhance the value of intangibles and develop a methodology to adequately measure such value. Particularly, brand is considered as the fifth major business resource after human resources, goods, money and information. Therefore, adequate valuation of the brand and the public disclosure are both significant challenges in pursuing an 'intangible business strategy', since they may help predict the firm's ability to generate future cash flows and thus enhance shareholder value.

Since July 2001, the Committee[1] has conducted a Questionnaire on Brand Valuation and performed intensive review and discussions from various aspects in a most comprehensive manner, spending approximately 200 hours over a wide range of issues such as the development of the Brand Valuation Model, the possible treatment of the brand royalty fee, how to fully utilise the results of the Questionnaire on Brand Valuation for brand management, disclosure of brands, and so forth.

Definition of brand

Since a brand is something to 'identify' and 'differentiate' itself with other companies or competing products and services, the Committee has decided to define 'brand' as 'emblems including names, logos, marks, symbols, package designs, and so forth used by companies to identify and differentiate their products and services from those of competitors'.

When companies become able to develop customer loyalty and trust in the products and services and maintain a continuous relationship with the customers through its brand, the customers will begin to make purchase decisions based on brand rather than physical or functional aspects of the products and services and, as a result, the brand will gain competitive advantage. Competitive advantage of a brand will be realised initially through price advantage, high degree of customer loyalty and brand expansion power, i.e. capability to expand the brand geographically as well as to expand into similar or different industries, and thus increase present and future cash flows for the company. Price advantage, mentioned above, means that products and services with a brand value are able to be sold at higher prices than those without a brand value but with identical quality and function. In other words, the brand may become a factor that generates greater present and future cash flows.

High degree of customer loyalty means that customers will purchase products and services with brands continuously and repeatedly over time and, therefore, generate stable and steady increases in the present and future cash flows.

With respect to brand expansion power, it means the ability to expand the market of the brand overseas and/or to stretch into markets of similar or different industries, and thus become a factor that increases present and future cash flow.

Brand royalty fees: current practice and issues

Brand royalty fee is generally described as the consideration that a user of a brand pays for the usage of the brand to the owner. There are basically two types of brand royalty fee. One is the brand royalty fee exchanged in the name of corporate mark usage fee or licence fee where companies that possess legal rights to exclusively use the brand and allow other parties to use the brand (referred to as 'brand usage permission fee', hereinafter). The other is charged within a particular corporate group in the name of 'group management operating fee' to cover the cost used for the maintenance, management, and development of brands used within the entire corporate group (referred to as 'brand management fee', hereinafter).

If there is no rationality in the payment and receipt of the brand royalty fee under the Commercial Code, there is a possibility that the directors of the company who are using the brand might be charged for damages and losses under the Commercial Code, and also be charged for any third party. When there are minority shareholders in subsidiaries of a company, there is a possibility that the rights and interests of the minority shareholders might be negatively infringed by transactions between the subsidiary and its parent. So there needs to be a rational explanation made to minority shareholders. If an exchange of the brand royalty fee is not considered rational, such a fee is subject to 'taxation for contribution' under the Corporation Tax Laws, and to 'transfer pricing' under the special Taxation Measures Law.

'Taxation for contribution' is a system that recognises a certain portion of a donation exceeding certain amounts as non-deductible. 'Transfer pricing' is a system that calculated the taxable income by recognising transactions with overseas affiliates as transactions between independent bodies at arm's length price.

In order to pay and receive a brand royalty fee, one must explain that such an exchange of fee is rational not only to the counter party of the affiliated companies, but also to the minority shareholders and their third parties from the Commercial Code perspective as well as to the tax authorities from the Corporation Tax Laws perspective. Therefore, it is necessary to calculate brand royalty fee based on an objective methodology excluding quantitative factors as much as possible.

Set out below is how to calculate the brand royalty fee, applying the Brand Valuation Model developed by the Committee.

Brand usage permission fee $= PD \times LD \times LD$
Brand Management Cost $= CBMC \times BP/CBP - BMC$

CBMC: Consolidated Brand Management Cost

CBP: Consolidated Brand Profit

BMC: Brand Management Cost paid by the individual company using corporate brand

BP: Brand Profit of the individual company using corporate brand

---

Capitalisation of brands: implications and issues

As the importance of brand as one of the key business resources increases, the number of companies that have few assets to be reported on the balance sheet has increased. However, from a practical point of view, capitalisation of brand has not necessarily been a common practice.

Classifying brand into 'purchased brand' and 'internally generated brand' and categorising the meaning of the brand by companies that issue securities (referred to as 'issuers', hereinafter) and by users of such information, the Committee could generally summarise the meaning of capitalising brand as follows.

The meaning of capitalising purchased brands from an issuer's perspective can be explained as follows. By clearly recognising and positioning the brand as one of the key business resources that generate future cash flows rather than treating them collectively in a black box as intangibles referred to as goodwill, a firm that is undervalued in the capital market may see an increase in its stock price thus increasing its market capitalisation value and enhancing its competitive advantage. By capitalising the brand, the company can explain the rationality of impairing goodwill that may not possess the feature of an asset as well as explain the efficiency of investments.

The meaning of capitalisation of purchased brands from the information user's perspective can be explained as follows. It makes it possible to recognise goodwill, often recognised as a black box, as the residual of net investment and, as a result, not only enables them to capture the efficiency of investment, but also clarifies the value of brand as one of the key business resources, and thus helps to utilise the information to predict future cash flows.

The meaning of capitalisation of internally generated brands on the issuers' perspective could be explained as follows. It will increase the importance of brand in business and business chances of companies with brand will increase. The basis for calculation of the brand royalty fee becomes clearer. Besides, it will clarify the potential capability to create future cash flows and corporate values in the form of market capitalisation, as well as shareholders' values, increase, thus enhancing competitiveness in the market leading to easier access to finance. Furthermore, it would make it possible not only to adequately analyse intangibles as the difference between total market value for corporate value, but prevent takeover bids ('TOBs') based on undervalued stock prices.

The meaning of capitalisation of internally generated brands on the information users' side could be explained as follows. By identifying internally generated brands as potential capability to create future cash flows, it will help predict the expected future cash flows, prospect of future corporate values as well as to enable adequate corporate valuation which may remove the information asymmetries. Besides, by capitalising internally generated brands by an objective methodology, its comparability would be secured and, as a result, its usefulness as the source of information for making investment decisions would be enhanced.

The reason why internally generated intangibles, as well as internally generated brands, have not been recognised as assets on the balance sheet is that the measurement of brand asset is not reliable, and that the amounts on creditors are regarded as unrealised gains. In relation to the Commercial Code, there are two issues described as follows. First, even in the case of trade mark rights protected by criminal penalties in addition to rights to recover damaged reputation, valuations of its value have been made carefully to avoid overvaluation of assets based on protection of its creditors. Second, the capitalisation of internally generated brand may not constitute income available for dividends, as is the case with business accounting.

The Committee considers that it is necessary to make measures in the area of dividend regulations under the Commercial Code to capitalise internally generated brands on a legal entity basis.

Brand Valuation Model

Generally speaking, approaches to valuation of intangibles including brands can be classified into 'residual approach' and 'independent valuation approach'. Strengths and weaknesses of these approaches are explained as follows.

'Residual approach' considers brand value as the result of subtracting the book value of all net assets on the balance sheet from the total value of the company described as the market capitalisation amount.

The strength of this approach is that it is based on market capitalisation, which could be seen as an objective measure, and calculation is relatively easy. On the other hand, the value calculated in this approach includes not only brands subject to valuation but also goodwill and other intangibles. Besides, assuming the market capitalisation amount as the overall value of the company may mean that accounting is using market data.

The 'independent valuation approach' values brand independently and could be classified broadly into 'cost approach', 'market approach' and 'income approach'.

Cost approach, which consists of 'historical cost approach' and 'replacement cost approach', values brand based on the cost spent in developing the brand. This approach has strength in its feasibility and usefulness for making comparisons; on the other hand, it also has weaknesses in that the relationship between cost and brand value is unclear and that historical cost paid to develop a brand as well as replacement value estimates may not be relevant to the value of a brand due to time gaps and correlation gaps.

Market approach values brand by making reference to the actual price of similar brands traded in the market. This approach may not be rational in assuming that similar brands will be priced alike and, additionally, there could be issues in objectivity raised by differences in actually traded price of brand.

Income approach values brands based on the net present value of the excess profit or future cash flows, and this is classified into 'royalty exemption method' and 'premium price method'. The Committee has decided to support this approach to determine the brand value.

The royalty exemption method measures excess profit by the royalty fee that a company would have to pay if it did not hold the brand. This cannot be used if there is no actual exchange of royalty fee, and it does not make sense referring to the royalty fee of other seemingly similar brands. The price premium method measures the excess of profit by the present and future price premium of branded products compared with products without brand. The Committee has decided to adopt this method.

The Committee has decided to calculate brand value based on the concept that brand value is described as a function of three drivers, i.e. Prestige, Loyalty and Expansion. Prestige Driver focuses on the price advantage created by the reliability of the brand that enables the company to sell the product constantly at higher prices compared with the competitor. Price advantage is explained by the excess value of branded products over that of non-branded products, and it becomes the basis for the increases in present and future cash flows generated by the brand (referred to as 'excess profits', hereinafter). Regarding the calculation of excess profits, the Committee decided to adopt 'sales differentials per cost of sales' as the unit price index. In determining the benchmark, the Committee adopted the method using the lowest figure in the same industry. As the method to calculate the portion of excess profits originated by brands, the Committee adopted the one to extract the profits originated by brands by using a certain ratio (referred to as 'brand attribution rate', hereinafter). Brand attribution rate is described as the proportion of development, maintenance and management cost related to brand (referred to as 'brand management cost', hereinafter) to the overall operational cost of a company. The formula for calculating the driver was decided as follows:

PD = Excess Profit Ratio × Brand Attribution Rate × Cost of Sales

= [5 year Average of {(Sales of the Company/Cost of Sales of the Company – Sales of a Benchmark Company/Cost of Sales of a Benchmark Company × Advertisement and Promotion Cost Ratio of the Company)} × Cost of Sales of the Company]

Loyalty Driver focuses on the capability of a brand to maintain stable sales for a long period based on stable clients or repeaters with high loyalty. The Committee decided to use the five-year average for the cost of sales and derive the average (μ) and standard deviation (σ), and defined Loyalty Driver by taking the proportion of the difference between standard deviation and average to the average. If the figure of cost of sales is stable, standard deviation should be small and the Loyalty Driver value described as $(\mu - \sigma)/\mu$ should become closer to 1. The formula for calculating Loyalty Driver has been decided as follows:

LD = (5-year Average Cost of Sales – 5-year Standard Deviation of
　　　Cost of Sales)/5-year Average Cost of Sales

　　　(= 1 – Volatility Coefficient of Cost of Sales)

$LD = (\mu C - \sigma C)/\mu C$

μC: 5-year average of cost of sales; σC: standard deviation of cost of
sales

Expansion Driver focuses on the fact that a brand with high status is recognised widely and, therefore, is capable of expanding from its traditional industry and markets to similar or different industries as well as to overseas expanding its market geographically. As the parameter for brand expansion power, the Committee adopted the average of 'the growth rate of the overseas sales' and 'the growth rate of sales in the non-core segment of the company'. The formula is as follows:

ED = Average Growth Rate of Overseas Sales and Growth Rate of
　　　Sales of Non-core Business Segments

$$ED = \frac{1}{2}\left\{ \frac{1}{2}\sum_{i=-1}^{0}\left(\frac{SO_i - SO_{i-1}}{SO_{i-1}} + 1 \right) + \frac{1}{2}\sum_{i=-1}^{0}\left(\frac{SX_i - SX_{i-1}}{SX_{i-1}} + 1 \right) \right\}$$

SO: Overseas Sales; SX: Sales of non-core business segments

(Note) Each indicator should not be smaller than 1

The model developed, based on the basic concept of Brand Valuation Model, is as follows:

$$BV = f(PD, LD, ED, r)$$
$$= PD/r \times LD \times ED$$

$$= \frac{\left[\frac{1}{5}\sum_{i=-1}^{0}\left\{ \left(\frac{S_i}{C_i} - \frac{S_i^*}{C_i^*} \right) \times \frac{A_i}{OE_i} \right\} \times C_0 \right]}{r} \times \frac{\mu_C - \sigma_C}{\mu_C}$$

$$\times \frac{1}{2}\left\{ \frac{1}{2}\sum_{i=-1}^{0}\left(\frac{SO_i - SO_{i-1}}{SO_{i-1}} + 1 \right) + \frac{1}{2}\sum_{i=-1}^{0}\left(\frac{SX_i - SX_{i-1}}{SX_{i-1}} + 1 \right) \right\}$$

PD = Excess Profit Ratio × Brand Attribution Rate × Cost of Sales

= Past 5-term Average of [(Sales/Cost of Sales of a Benchmark Company/Cost of Sales of a Benchmark Company) × Advertising and Promotion Cost Ratio (Cost of Brand Management*)] × Cost of Sales

LD = (Cost of Sales μ – Cost of Sales σ)/Cost of Sales μ

(Note) μ and σ are calculated based on the past 5-term data of Cost of Sales

ED = Average of Overseas Growth Rate and Sales Growth Rate of Non-core Business Segment

(Note) Minimum value of each index should be 1

S:	Sales	S^*:	Sales of a Benchmark Company
C:	Cost of Sales (CS)	C^*:	Cost of Sales of a Benchmark Company
A:	Advertising and Promotion Cost (Cost of Brand Management*)	OE:	Operating Cost
μC:	5-term average of CS	σC:	Standard Deviation of CS
SO:	Overseas Sales	SX:	Non-core Business Segment Sales
r:	Discount rate		

*: If one can ensure the credibility of figures through assurance of an independent audit, it is desirable to use Brand Management Cost as the input

Brand Management Model

While brand value is becoming more important in corporate management, it is extremely important to enhance the value of brands in the management focusing on brands (referred to as 'brand management', hereinafter). The Committee suggests a new Brand Management Model in order to maximise the brand value, functionally integrating brand value board and brand value chart. The brand value chart has the following characteristics: (1) it incorporates financial and management organisational perspectives; (2) it incorporates financial and non-financial indicators into the valuation to evaluate its activity and the effects form various angles; and (3) it establishes a feedback loop to further refine brand strategy.

In order to further promote and encourage brand management practice of companies, the Committee proposes to define key items that enhance brand value as brand fundamentals, and disclose its conceptual framework to external stakeholders.

Disclosure of brand assets

In order to account for brands as assets on the balance sheet, it is necessary to clarify standards to be recognised on financial statements. The issue is based on the recognition criteria from Statements of Financial Accounting Concepts ('SFAC') developed by FASB.

According to SFAC, the criteria for recognition of assets are described as follows: they should meet (1) the 'definitions' of an element of financial statements; (2) the 'measurability' criterion; (3) the 'relevance' criterion; and (4) the 'reliability' criterion. First of all, the 'definitions' above are described as follows. Assets are probable future economic benefits obtained or controlled by a particular entity as a result of past transactions or events. As is clear from this definition, in order for brands to be accounted for as assets, the following three requirements should be met. The first characteristic of assets is the existence (or the non-existence) of a 'future economic benefit'. Economic benefit is interpreted as being something that eventually results in cash flows to the business enterprises. Given the fact that a brand is a typical value driver and is a source for future cash flows, it does meet the first criterion. The second characteristic is that the economic benefit should be attributable to a specific entity. In the case of brands, this is met given that they are attributable to companies as corporate brands or product brands, and are independently recognised from brands of other companies. The third characteristic is 'occurrence of past transaction of event'. This is a requirement to distinguish between the future economic benefits of present and future assets of an entity. Given a brand is usually developed over a long time span and is likened to the current brand it does meet this third criterion as well. Therefore, given that brand possesses each of those three essential characteristics, it meets the assets definition.

The second criterion for recognition, 'measurability', is explained in that the information on financial statements has to be quantified in monetary units with sufficient reliability. Under SFAC, it refers to five different attributes used under current accounting practices; namely, historical cost, current cost, current market value, net realisable value and present value of future cash flows. In addition, it also refers to expected cash flows as an extension of current market value and this has been used in the Brand Valuation Model adopted by the Committee.

The third criterion, 'relevance', is explained as the information about it that is capable of making a difference in user decisions. Therefore, in order for certain information to be recognised on the financial statements, such information needs to have 'relevance' for the user, and must have feedback value or predictive value for users, and timeliness. In the case of brands, it satisfies the 'relevance' criteria both from the issuers' side as well as the users' side.

The fourth criterion, 'reliability', is explained as the information being representative, faithful, verifiable and neutral.

The Committee considers that the Brand Valuation Model and the results proposed by the Committee both meet the above criteria to be recognised as an asset on the balance sheet, at least conceptually.

Even with the assumption that all requirements are met, there is a need to further discuss how these items should be publicly disclosed. Set out below are three ways of public disclosure under the Japanese business corporate accounting system. The first proposition is to recognise brands on the consolidated balance sheet under the current financial reporting system. The Committee believes that there are no significant issues in this idea under the current corporate financial accounting principle considering that the function of it has shifted from coordinating various interests of stakeholders to providing information. The second proposition is to disclose brands under notes or supplementary information sections as a step-by-step approach. The third proposition is to disclose them as part of business reporting regardless of the current financial reporting system. This is a new paradigm reporting including a wide range of information, such as forecasts information, company's basic objective, strategy and so forth.

Enhancing the value of brand

The brand, itself, comprises various perspectives and would be a vital element for investment. According to Mr Warren Buffett, the successful American investor, industries consist of two types of companies, i.e. a small minority of the first-class companies that are worth investing in and huge numbers of the second-class companies that are entirely worthless of long-term investment. He also insists that the key which determines whether a company can be first class or not depends on the fact that it is a 'business franchise'. In other words, it is in the situation prior to other competitors and has not been threatened by new companies in sales prices and profit.

The idea of enhancing the value of brand is expected to be an important element for business strategy in the near future and, in this sense, this report, having been released globally, will be a milestone for the industrial world, not just Japan.

Towards a nation built on intellectual property

To understand the impetus behind the drive for such intensive study on brand valuation, it is important to understand Prime Minister Koizumi's speech 'The Basic Law on Intellectual Property' of February 2002 which laid the foundations of Japan's drive to invent its way out of economic inertia. As Prime Minister Koizumi was re-elected in early November 2003 there is now a political mandate to continue to press forward with the reforms that he has helped to initiate.

Prime Minister Koizumi declared that Japan would be a nation built on intellectual property in his policy speech in February 2002. The Japanese government established the Intellectual Property Strategy Committee in March 2002 and published the *Intellectual Property Policy Outline* in July 2002. Only nine months after Prime Minister Koizumi's speech, the Basic Law on Intellectual Property was enacted. Such quick actions mean that Japan is keen to be a nation built on intellectual property. 'A nation that is built on intellectual property' means establishing a nation where intellectual property is used to create high-value added products and services with the aim of revitalising the economy and society (see Figure 6).

The Japanese government recently revised its estimates of real economic growth in the second quarter of 2003 to 1.0 per cent from 0.6 per cent. The revision means Japan's quarterly growth rate was faster than growth in both the US and Europe. Also, a surge in investment by Japanese firms boosted growth in the April–June quarter to its current level for two and a half years, and economists say Japan's cyclical recovery has further to run. It is too early to say that stronger growth is being caused by structural reforms, and Japan is continuing to make great efforts to implement various reforms, especially in the field of IP.

Reassessment of brand valuation is one important aspect of such reform as noted at the beginning of this chapter.

Key Points toward the Realisation of an Intellectual Property-based Nation

Strengthen Efforts towards the Worldwide Patent Granting System
Promote Mutual Exploitation of Search Results between Japan and US
initiate a near term project within 2002
Draw up a Plan to Ensure Examination for Timely and High quality patents within 2002

Creation of 'Patent Specialised Court' Function
Concentrate Patent-related Lawsuits at Tokyo or Osaka District Courts
submit amendment bill in 2003

Strengthen Measures Against Counterfeit and Pirate Products
Strengthen Border Measures against Infringing Products
improve legislation operation by FY2004
Strengthen Approaches through International Negotiation, etc. in and after 2002

Strengthen Trade Secret Protection
Strengthen Protection in Civil and Criminal Aspects submit amendment bill in 2003

Strengthen IP Creation and Management Capability in Universities
Establish System to Strategically Create IP in Cooperation with Corporations by FY2003
Establish Intellectual Property Departments in tens of Universities start by FY2003

Foster Intellectual Property Specialists
Enrich Intellectual Property Education in Law Schools
scheduled to start admitting students in and after FY2004

Figure 6

1 Outline of Prime Minister Koizumi's policy speech

Prime Minister Koizumi made his Administrative Policy Speech on 4 February 2002, stating that:

> Japan has already produced intellectual properties of the finest class in the world. I have set the national goal of strengthening the international competitiveness of the Japanese industry through strategically protecting and utilising the achievements in researches and creative activities as our intellectual property. To this end, Japan will establish the Intellectual Property Strategy Committee and forcefully promote necessary policies.

2 *Intellectual Property Policy Outline*

The Intellectual Property Strategy Committee which was established in the Prime Minister's Cabinet Office published the *Intellectual Property Policy Outline* in July 2002. (Key points are in Figure 7.)

4 Basic Law on Intellectual Property

The Basic Law on Intellectual Property was enacted in September 2002 (enforced on 1 March 2003). (Outline of the Law is in Figure 8.)

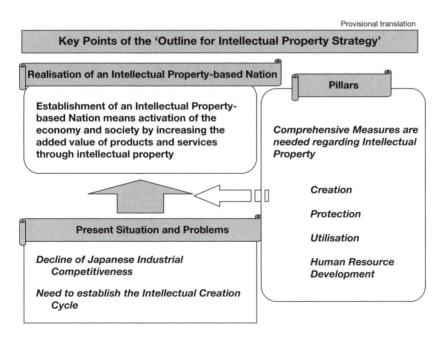

Provisional translation

Key Points of the 'Outline for Intellectual Property Strategy'

Realisation of an Intellectual Property-based Nation

Establishment of an Intellectual Property-based Nation means activation of the economy and society by increasing the added value of products and services through intellectual property

Present Situation and Problems

Decline of Japanese Industrial Competitiveness

Need to establish the Intellectual Creation Cycle

Pillars

Comprehensive Measures are needed regarding Intellectual Property

Creation

Protection

Utilisation

Human Resource Development

Figure 7

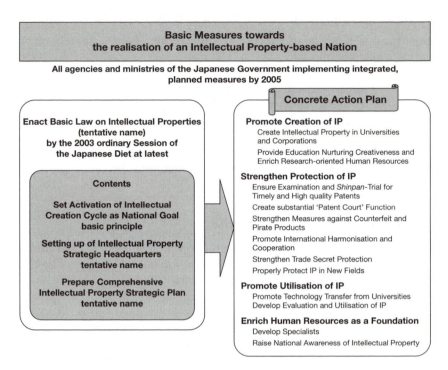

Figure 8

5 Intellectual Property Strategic Programme

The Intellectual Property Headquarters (Director-General: Prime Minister Koizumi) was established in March 2003 and the Japanese government announced the Intellectual Property Strategic Programme in July 2003. Key points are below:

(1) Creation of IP
- Expansion of the national subsidies to acquisition and management of intellectual property rights at universities
- Abolition or amendment of the Employee's Invention Rules

(2) Protection of IP
- Enactment of the Faster Patent Examination Law (provisional name)
- Expansion of the patent subjects to medical practice
- Study on the establishment of the Intellectual Property High Court
- Study on the establishment of the International Intellectual Property Trade Committee (provisional name) to counter infringements

(3) Utilisation of IP
  • Utilisation of the trust system for management and mobility of intellectual property

(4) Expansion of the contents industry
  • Diversification of fund procurement methods and financial support

(4) Education
  • Education of attorneys specialising in intellectual property
  • Promotion of the establishment of a graduate school, Management of Technology (MOT).

5 Measures by industrial property administration to meet the new age

1 Fast and accurate examination and judgement

Realisation of fast and accurate examination and judgement is a priority mission in industrial property administration as pointed out in the *Intellectual Property Policy Outline*. At patent examinations, in particular, the Japan Patent Office (JPO) will wrestle with the important issue of ensuring promptness in granting rights while maintaining the high quality of examination.

(1) Prompt granting of rights

Among the various procedures related to industrial property, the JPO shall first speed up the filing documents for the formality examination and registration of the industrial property.

To speed up the patent examination, it is important to establish a broad system capable of meeting diversified needs since the necessity for examination speed differs for each applicant in each field of technology. The JPO shall endeavour to structure an efficient examination processing system because it is taken for granted that the examination starts as quickly as possible after an applicant submits a request for one. The JPO shall further generalise an accelerated examination that significantly shortens the waiting time for applications by universities, small- and medium-sized enterprises and venture companies, patent applications that are also filed overseas, and patent applications that are certain to be executed. Promptness of granting a patent is particularly required in those cases, and the JPO shall actively promote utilisation of this accelerated examination to the applicants. The JPO shall also set a quantitative target for the period from the application for an accelerated examination to notification of the result of the primary examination and shall process the applications quickly. The JPO shall also proactively execute circuit examinations with the objective of supporting small- and medium-sized enterprises, venture companies, etc. in all areas of Japan.

As for the design examination, the JPO shall set a quantitative target for the period of the accelerated examination for those applications that particularly require early processing because the need for faster granting of rights is higher as the product cycle becomes shorter.

As for the trademark examination, the JPO shall observe the provision to complete the primary examination within 18 months for all cases. For applications for accelerated examination that urgently require granting of rights, the JPO shall set a quantitative target for the period from the filing of the application to notification of the result of the primary examination and shall process them quickly.

(2) Accurate granting of rights

The JPO shall execute the procedures of the formality examination and industrial property registration properly and accurately, endeavour to achieve stable operation of the online reception system and take every precaution to prevent causing accidental inconvenience to the applicants. At substantive examinations, the JPO shall endeavour to achieve equal and stable granting of rights by reviewing the correction limits and other examination standards and by ensuring that everyone is thoroughly familiar with the examination standards. Specifically, the JPO shall thoroughly investigate prior-art examples, issue proper judgement to ensure objectivity of the results of substantive examinations and reduce the number of reversals at subsequent trials for invalidation in order to be able to grant highly reliable and stable rights. The JPO shall also reorganise the examination-related information system to establish an environment for prompt and accurate examinations.

(3) Prompt and efficient intellectual property dispute processing

The JPO reviewed the relationship between the opposition system and trial for the invalidation system based on the Intellectual Property Policy Plan and submitted the bill to the ordinary Diet session this year for unification into a new trial system for invalidation that has the benefits of both systems. The JPO shall strive for proper operation of the judgement system by simplifying and streamlining it and shall reorganise the functions required by the Intellectual Property Policy Plan in observance of the results of the deliberation of the subject bill at the Diet. The JPO shall ensure that anyone demanding a trial appeal has thorough knowledge of the new system.

(4) Support for creation of excellent designs and brands, and their strategic utilisation

The significant elements in strengthening industrial competitiveness are creation, protection and utilisation of attractive designs and brands as well as promotion of technological development. The JPO, therefore, shall study the policy to promote utilisation of design- and brand-related information in its possession and prepare a bill within this fiscal year in order to promote structuring and creation of attractive designs and brands. The JPO shall also study the design and trademark systems to decide on specific policies for establishing an environment to offer products and services with higher value by utilising attractive designs and brands by FY2005. The JPO shall review the ideal method for protection of designs (which will also involve a process of valuation) to be utilised in the network as soon as possible and reach a conclusion within fiscal year 2003. The information-oriented society is rapidly progressing.

2 Measures against unauthorised copies in Japan

The JPO shall promote stronger cooperation with the customs houses to effectively prevent inflow of unauthorised copies to Japan.

3 Proper protection of intellectual property overseas

Damages incurred from infringement of intellectual property rights by unauthorised copies, etc. are increasing mainly in the Asian regions and seriously impacting the activities of Japanese enterprises. The JPO shall, therefore, firmly request preparation of laws, establishment of a system and improvement of its operations against unauthorised copies to the countries and regions in Asia through bilateral and multilateral negotiations and strengthen international cooperation on protection of intellectual property jointly with European countries and the US. Following the joint mission of the Government and people to China last December, the JPO shall pro-actively support activities for the protection of IPR of the Japanese industry overseas in close cooperation with the International Intellectual Property Protection Forum.

4 International accord in the intellectual property system

(1) International accord and strengthening of efforts for cooperation in examinations

It is necessary to file the same application in overseas countries in order to acquire international rights, and applicants are suffering from the heavy burden of the extra procedure and expense. The responsibilities of patent offices in all countries are rapidly increasing because the same applications must be examined. The JPO shall promote cooperation among world-wide patent offices, including correlative utilisation of prior-art search results and examination results, with due consideration to the sovereignty of each country, in order to make the application process smoother and to reduce the number of responsibilities. The JPO shall lead discussions on the reformation of the Patent Cooperation Treaty (PCT) in the World Intellectual Property Organisation (WIPO) to enhance the efficiency of the system and the convenience for applicants, and take active measures in discussions on the Substantive Patent Law Treaty (SPLT) at WIPO to achieve international accord in the patent system. As for the designs, the JPO shall endeavour to establish a system in which the 'primary examination is conducted within 12 months for all cases' as provided in the Hague Agreement Geneva Act (adopted in July 1999, but not yet effective) and review compliance to the Act. In regard to trademarks, the trilateral trade-mark meetings of the Japan Patent Office, the United States Patent and Trademark Office (USPTO) and Office for Harmonisation in the Internal Market (OHIM) shall review issues regarding the indications of product and usage names, Vienna figure classification, and so forth, in order to reduce the burden of examination responsibilities of the three offices and to enhance convenience for the applicants, and to promote international accord in the trademark system.

The number of participating countries in the Protocol Relating to the Madrid Agreement Concerning the International Registration of Marks, an international system for trademark registration, has exceeded that of the Madrid Agreement and further increase is expected. It is inevitable that applications for trademark registration in the framework of this Protocol will increase and the JPO, therefore, will take active measures to achieve international accord in the trademark system to make the Protocol even easier for applicants to utilise. The JPO shall also make efforts in conducting a review for the amendment of the Trademark Law Treaty (TLT) and substantive accord of the trademark system at the standing committee for laws on trademarks, designs and geographical displays at WIPO and strive to achieve international accord.

(2) Smoother acquisition of international rights through international accord on the patent examination standards

As the patent examination standards in Japan are somewhat different from those in Europe and the US, review and promotion of international accord on the patent examination standards will enable protection of rights over a wide global spectrum and also make it easier for Japanese enterprises to acquire international rights. The JPO shall review the correction limits, clearly describe the specification requirements and make other revisions in the patent examination standards in order to properly protect the rights, promote international accord and enhance expectancy of acquisition of rights in FY2003. As for the international accord on the singularity requirement for inventions, it is included in the Patent Law Amendment Bill submitted to the Diet. After amendment, the JPO shall endeavour to establish patent examination standards that protect the rights in a proper range with international accord.

(3) Support for establishment of the system and enforcement in Asia

The JPO shall utilise JICA and other bilateral schemes or WIPO and other multilateral schemes to dispatch specialists, hold on-site seminars, receive trainees, cooperate in education and collaborate on information-oriented technology building. These efforts shall support the legal structure and its operational system for intellectual property in countries and regions of Asia. The JPO shall also start a service to announce the examination results in Japan through the Internet in English for the patent offices in Asia to contribute to prompt granting of rights in Asia.

5 Protection of intellectual property in new fields

After the Basic Science and Technology Plan decided by the Cabinet meeting in March 2001, applicants have gained a higher level of awareness on the importance of acquisition of patents in the eight fields, including the four priority fields, presented in the Plan (life-science, data communication, environment, nanotechnology and its materials, energy, manufacturing technology, social foundation and frontier). Supporting the acquisition of rights in those fields should promote strategic research and development as well as intellectual property management at enterprises and universities and contribute to the reinforcement of the industrial competitiveness of Japan. Therefore, the JPO shall promptly establish examination standards for proper protection of rights in those fields, and it is important for the JPO to publicise the patent information in its possession after appropriate investigation and analysis.

(1) Establishment of examination standards for the field of frontier science and technology

The JPO made drastic amendments to the examination standards including the establishment of examination standards for gene-related inventions and business system related inventions in FY2000. In FY2002, the JPO prepared a sample collection of inventions related to the stereoscopic structure of protein. The JPO shall continue to reorganise and fulfil the examination standards for proper acquisition of rights in the field of frontier science and technology.

(2) Promotion of providing data for the eight fields including the four priority fields

Investigation and analysis of the patent information in the frontier science and technology fields should have further renewal impact by enabling investment in effective research and development and avoiding duplicate researches. The JPO, therefore, shall conduct surveys on technological trends by utilising the patent information, disclose the results, periodically announce the numbers of disclosures and registration of patent applications concerning the eight fields including the four priority fields, and make efforts to offer timely and high-quality information.

6 Review on employees' invention system

Frequent disputes have been occurring recently between employers and former employees concerning the 'corresponding compensation' for inventions by employees as employment practices change and the views of employees at departments of research change from the traditional way of thinking. The JPO, therefore, shall review whether amendment is necessary and, if so, in which direction it should be headed, based on the results of surveys conducted last year on the actual conditions at enterprises, views of the employees and systems and actual conditions of foreign countries. Due consideration shall be given to ensuring incentives to inventors for research and development, reduction of patent management cost and risk at enterprises, and reinforcement of the industrial competitiveness of Japan, and the JPO shall reach a conclusion by the end of FY2003.

7 Providing information

The JPO shall endeavour to establish an environment with smoother procedures for the applicants by holding meetings to explain industrial property application procedures and re-organisation of functions for applications via PC because it is important to enhance the convenience of the applicants in order to provide proper protection and promote utilisation of industrial property rights. The JPO shall also promote international standardisation of the application format to make it even easier for the applicants, systematically develop and establish a data system, and promote international standardisation of the gazette format. The JPO shall offer more information related to the industrial property rights system on the web site and take positive actions in offering industrial property rights information electronically as the intelligence technology-oriented trend progresses.

As for the Industrial Property Digital Library, the JPO plans to improve accessibility based on standard usage by the general public through updating of its hardware. The JPO shall also take positive actions to become capable of offering the data in XML format and other forms that are more convenient for users, in an effort to offer industrial property information electronically.

8 Promotion of education

The JPO shall offer materials for teaching the basics of the intellectual property system and shall also hold more seminars for students and teachers to nurture awareness and further support intellectual property rights education at primary and secondary schools and at universities, etc. The JPO shall also promote various seminars on the industrial property rights system for enterprises at different locations throughout the nation to popularise and generalise the system, and endeavour to educate people to be fully able to utilise the intellectual property rights system. The JPO shall gather statistics on the utilisation condition of the intellectual property system and proactively develop patent distribution promotion activities in close cooperation with the National Centre for Industrial Property Information.

9 Consultation service to enhance satisfaction of the users

The JPO shall establish an environment where applicants, etc. can submit applications more easily and with greater satisfaction through the establishment of a system in which officers who hold thorough knowledge of the various procedures for industrial property rights offer consultation services. At this time, JPO officers shall offer kind and courteous consultations to the users in close cooperation with the consultation service at the independent administrative corporation, the National Centre for Industrial Property Information. The JPO shall also establish a system to receive the opinions of users worldwide regarding the administrative service of the JPO.

10 Collection of opinions of external learned persons

Upon execution of the industrial property rights administration, the JPO shall reflect the users' opinions and also request opinions from external learned persons through substantial utilisation of consulting firms and other outside investigation organisations.

Concluding remarks

Within only one-and-a-half years of Prime Minister Koizumi's speech in February 2002, the Japanese government has promoted a high number of policies on intellectual property. These activities demonstrate that it is possible to carry out reforms in Japan. But the way to a nation built on intellectual property is both steep and sharp.

Japanese international competitiveness is closely linked with the strength of IP. Japanese attempts towards a nation built on intellectual property is one of essential key factors which will determine the future of Japan.

Note

1 This refers to the Ministry for Economy, Trade and Industry (METI) Report on Brand Evaluation of June 2002, 140 pp., and subsequent material is also drawn from the Supreme Court Ruling of April 2003.

9   Japanese patent publications as a source of information

Steve Van Dulken

Japanese patents have a formidable reputation because of the language barrier for most Westerners. A less obvious problem is the problem of numeration. This chapter is about ways of finding and using the published materials to obtain information and is written primarily for the Westerner with little or no understanding of Japanese or of patent publications. It is a reworking of the Japanese chapter from the book *Introduction to Patents Information*[1] with some additional material and does not pretend to cover the entire field, which is complicated enough for Western patents, let alone Japanese. Ideally, expert advice or searching should be requested. Even so, a little effort can reveal a great deal of technical and business information even for someone who does not know any Japanese.

In 2001 there were over 430,000 applications filed in Japan for patents of which less than 9 per cent were by foreigners. About 120,000 patents were registered (granted). These numbers are very large by Western standards as Japanese industry is very keen to patent. There are also utility models, which provide a lesser level of protection. These were formerly equally numerous, but only 9,000 were registered in that year because of changes in the patent laws. Relatively few Japanese inventions are published in English by patenting for foreign protection. In 2000 under 7,000 were granted (mostly in English) through the European Patent Convention while about 30,000 were granted in the US.

Patenting procedure

Japan publishes the unexamined patent application, usually referred to as a '*kokai*', or 'A', 18 months after the initial filing or 'priority date'. This would have occurred in Japan if the application was by a Japanese applicant, in say the US or Britain if it was a foreign applicant. Applications filed before 1971 were only published once as an examined application, where the Patent Office had decided if it was a new invention. Until 2001 the applicant had seven years from the date of filing before examination had to be asked for (this is now three years). If it is acceptable to the Patent Office, it is published a second time as a registered or granted (*toroku*) specification. Formerly there was an intermediate examined (*kokoku*) stage, but from May 1996 these stages have been combined. Any search reports listing similar patents will be printed on the front page of the second stage document at field (56). The citations are normally to other Japanese patent documents.

Formerly there was pre-grant opposition before the third *toroku* stage. A six-month opposition period is available after the second stage to enable others to complain that the patent ought not to be allowed. Granting or registering, itself, is dependent on the applicant asking for examination, and it was normal to wait during the seven-year period allowed to block others in the technology, who would be uncertain if the concept would be allowed. Some applicants are taking advantage of the ability to ask for a quick examination (if reasons are given) in which cases the second stage is, in fact, published as the only specification.

The patent term from 1995 was 20 years from first filing in Japan. Pending or existing patents on that date also had 20 years. Formerly the term was 15 years from publication of the B2 if no more than 20 years had elapsed from the filing date.

Utility models formerly had a similar procedure to that of the patents. The U documents are now normally published within months of the application being made as a single stage.

Numeration and document codes

Japanese patent numeration is very complicated and until recently a number could, in theory, refer to six different series. It usually consists of two (sometimes three or four) elements: (sometimes a prefix for the reign), a prefix for the year, a number (and sometimes a document code). It is dangerous to omit any information and any known citations should always be copied as given, and to verify the number any extra information (such as the subject, or the name of the applicant) should always be noted. The source of the data should also be noted in case of queries.

The first element is the name given to the Emperor's reign. The Emperor Hirohito ruled from 1925 to January 1989 and his reign was called *Showa*, usually shortened to S. In January 1989 the Emperor Akihito came to the throne and his reign is called *Heisei*, usually shortened to H. This element is often not given in citations. Some databases use numbers rather than letters, hence 3 for S and 4 for H (with earlier reigns being *Meiji*, 1, and *Taisho*, 2).

The second element is an indication of the year. Until 1996 (for second stage examined specifications) or 2000 (for published applications) this was a number which indicated the number of years since the beginning of the Emperor's reign. Filing numbers still use this system. Hence, a number in the first weeks of 1989 (just before the Emperor Hirohito's death) was prefixed by 64 as that was the sixty-fourth year of his reign. The remainder of 1989 was Year 1 of the Emperor Akihito's reign, a numeration which continued to be used until largely superseded after the end of 1999 (in which year it had reached Year 11). In 1996 the third stage grants began to be numbered in a continuous series beginning with 2,500,001, while from 2000 the published applications began to use Western years in annual sequences, hence 2000, 2001 and so on.

The third element is the actual number assigned to the specification. This is a number which begins for each series of numbers with 1 in the year (either Imperial or Western) in question and which began a fresh sequence the following year, though sometimes there is a continuous numeration.

The final element is a document code. The published applications are coded A while the published grants are coded B2 (but if published just the once following swift examination are coded B1). This element is sometimes omitted. Hence, 2003 publications could be correctly cited as JP 2000–148694A and JP 3422799 B2 although, in practice, Japanese publications sometimes vary. An initial 'P' may be used to indicate a patent. The differences with utility models are explained further on in this section.

Chemical Abstracts cites Japanese published applications as e.g. 'Jpn. Kokai Tokkyo Koho JP 2001 122,639' which helps to identify it as an A specification (although cited in the printed number index as an A2). *Kokai* means 'unexamined' and is frequently used as shorthand to mean a Japanese A specification. *Tokkyo Koho* means 'patent gazette'.

The second stage of publication used to be the middle stage, and was called *kokoku* ('examined'). These specifications were coded B2. The final stage was of registered or *toroku* ('registered') specifications which were numbered in a continuous series. From 29 May 1996 the final stage was abolished (although used for earlier applications) and was incorporated in the previously middle, second stage which began to be numbered from 2,500,001 onwards and are now called *toroku* (registered), the old name for the third stage (which had a continuous numeration). They are normally coded B2 but some are published for the first time (omitting the *kokai* stage) when they are coded as B1 specifications.

Table 1 explains how numbers can expect to be seen.

Utility models were formerly numbered in an identical format to the patents, with abbreviated versions of the specifications, coded as U, as the

Table 1

Year first affected	Filing numbers	Published A	Published B	Third, registered stage
1989	64-1 etc. or 1-1 etc.	64-1 etc. or 1-1 etc.	64-1 etc. or 1-1 etc.	1,471,001 etc.
1996	7-1 etc.	7-1 etc.	2,500,001 etc.	(abolished)
2000	12-1 etc.	2001-1 etc.	2,996,501 etc.	

first stage, and Y specifications as the second stage. They too had a registered stage numbered in a sequence which reached 1,738,000 in 1989. The U specifications were called *Jitsuyo shinan koho*.

From 26 July 1994 the old Y stage and the registered stage were abolished (although earlier filings continue to appear as Ys). There is now only the full specification, with the code U, which is numbered in a 3,000,001 onwards continuous series. From 5 June 1996 the remaining Ys were numbered in a 2,500,001 onwards series. Formerly, utility models were popular, but law changes have meant that less than 10,000 are now published annually.

Amended documents have different codes. If a B2 is reissued with amendments it is coded H. If a U is reissued with amendments it is coded I.

Numbers within the 500,001 onwards range of the published unexamined *kokai* applications within each year are used for translations of Patent Cooperation Treaty (PCT) applications that designate Japan. Numbers within the 700,001 onwards range of the published unexamined *kokai* applications within each year are used for Supplementary Protection Certificates for extensions of terms for pharmaceutical patents.

Inpadoc data, used widely in priced databases, cites B2 documents as B4 documents. Derwent Information, another source of priced data, in its databases and publications uses the last two digits of the Western year instead of the Japanese year to indicate the old examined, B2 series. Hence, for example, 97 was used for Imperial Year 9 (1997). Newly published Japanese numbers are getting much easier to understand. Formerly a number like 5-20000 could be any of six sequences (patent filing, utility model filing, A, B, U or Y). Now 12-20000 can only be either a patent filing or a utility model filing. Most requests are for the A, *kokai* specifications, otherwise for the B, *toroku*.

If there is uncertainty, clues are that unexamined applications have only been published since 1970 so 44 or lower *Showa* years can only be the examined stage (if not a filing number). Examined documents before 1996 never numbered above 89,000, so higher numbers will clearly be for filings or unexamined applications. If the enquirer is uncertain then the citation can be looked up on the Web to see if the abstract or drawings look right.

Derwent Information, who provide a huge, international priced database, has adopted the practice on its databases of using the Japanese year for applications and the last two digits of the Western year as a prefix for the examined stage of publication so that they could be distinguished.

Specifications

As with Western patent specifications, Japanese patents consist of a description of how the invention works, together with drawings if necessary, plus claims outlining the monopoly requested or granted. From 1994 only electronic formats were used to publish Japanese specifications, either on

(19) 汉体书写信息 (JP)　　　　(12) 汉体书写信息技术标准相 汉体书 (A)　　　　(11) 支援服务升级资讯

面简单 2000-148694
(P2000-148694A)

(43) 无线上 (12) 网 (5) 无 (30) 制 (2000.5.30)

(51) Int.Cl.^{7}	容档案下	FI		快速无 (快速)
G06F 15/02	500	G06F 15/02	500A	5B019
	335		335E	5E501
	345		345K	5K011
	654	3/00	654D	
	656		656D	

载使用界　作创　空间快速无 7　OL　(汉21写)　写信息技写

(21) 档案下载　　容档案下 10-316460

(22) 用界面简　　无线10单11容6 (1998.11.6)

(71) 容档案　395015319
汉体书写信息技术标准相汉体书写信息
容档案下载
服务升级资讯 7-1-1

(72) 写信息　支援　作创
容档案下载使用界面简单创 5-8

(74) 意空　100101867
支援服　息技　服务

F汉体书(案下)　5B019　GA00　HD20　JA10
　　　　　　　 5E501　AA05　AA11　AA17　BA20　CA04
　　　　　　　　　　　 CB03　FA13　FB03　FB28　FB32
　　　　　　　 5K011　JA01　JA03

(54) [技术标准相]　汉体书写信息技术标准相 汉体书写信息技术

(57) [术标]
[载使业]　作创意空间快速无线上网 作创意空间快速无
作创意空间快速无线上网作创
[速无线上网]　支援服务升级资讯专业制支援服务升级资
容档案下载使用界面简单支援服务升级资讯专业制用界面
容档案下载使用界面简单支援服务升级资讯专业制用界面
容档案下载使用界面简单支援服务升级资讯专业制用界面
容档案下载使用界面简单支援服务升级资讯专业制用界面
容档案下载使用界面简单支援服务升级资讯专业制用界面
容档案下载使用界面简单支援服务升级资讯专业制用界面
容档案下载使用界面简单支援服务升级资讯专业制用界面
容档案下载使用界面简单支援服务升级资讯专业制用界面
容档案下载使用界面简单支援服务升级资讯专业制用界面
无线上网

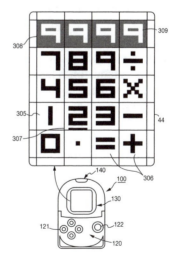

Figure 9

CD-ROM (DVD from 2004) or on the Web, and paper was no longer used. Figure 9 gives the front page of the unexamined application JP P2000-148694A. It is more prominently numbered as 2000-148694. This information is given at the top right of the page.

The numbers in brackets are used internationally to help interpret dates, numbers and names. The fact that the specification is actually Japanese is indicated by the country code (JP) at top left, code (19). The fact that it is an 'A' document is given at the top in the middle at code (12). The date of publication is given at code (43) at the top right, in this case 30 May 2000. In the illustrated front page, just above the second horizontal line, to the right, is '7' with a '21' with some Japanese within brackets. The 7 means the number of claims as given on page 2. The 21 indicates the number of pages in the specification. Formerly the number of pages was often two or three, but the specifications are becoming longer. No search report details are given but there is an abstract and (usually) a drawing. If the applicant and inventor details are for Westerners, the names are given in Western as well as Japanese characters.

The remainder of the patent specification follows a pattern. The claims come first, numbered within brackets in the format [1], [2], etc. There follows an explanation of earlier 'prior art' and the description, given in paragraphs in the format [0001], [0002], etc. Non-Japanese speakers will benefit from recognising the character for 'drawing'. This character is normally followed by the drawing number. If looking at the drawings shows that no. 25 is important, then the relevant paragraphs referring to it can be sent for translation or can be looked at in the automatic translations. The last part of the text, before the drawings, consists of numbered references explaining what each drawing is followed by a list of what the numbers on the drawings stand for. There may be occasional words in Roman characters. Typically these are Latin words or specialist technical terms. JP 2000-148694 for example has phrases such as 'SPU: Sound Processing Unit' and 'DMA: Direct Processing Unit' as helpful hints about what the paragraph is about.

Second stage specifications lack the front page drawings that the *kokai* have. An example is shown in Figure 10. On the left-hand side, field (21) gives the initial filing number, 4-192241, and (65) the published *kokai* number, 6-37692. The search report is on the right-hand side as field (58) and shows one 'A' and one 'U' document cited against it, suggesting that they are fairly similar (but not similar enough to disallow the patent). It only has one claim, [1], followed by the initial paragraph of the description, [0001].

Utility models will not have a description and are sometimes referred to as '*Jitsuyo shinan koho*' (their Japanese name). More information on interpreting Japanese specifications for chemists who know some of the language is in *Guide to Reading Japanese Patents*.[2]

(19) 汉体书写信息 (J P)　　　(12) 支 援 升 服 (B 2)　　　(11) 用界面简

援服务3100002支
(P3100002)

(46) 汉体单 支援12简8网16务(2000.8.16)　　　(19) 汉体单 支援12简8网18务(2000.8.18)

(21) Int. Cl⁷	升级资讯	P I		
H 0 4 B　7/26		H 0 4 B　7/26	J	
G 0 6 F　17/60		G 0 6 F　17/60	C	

速无线上网1(升 级 资)

(21)下载使用	汉体书写 – 192241	(23)下载使用	000237592
			汉体书写信息技术
(21) 载使用	快速无线 7信 20书(1992.7.20)		容档案下载使用界面简单支1档界 2档28 档
(65) 载使用网	速无线 6 – 37692	(72) 使用界	作创 作创
(43) 息技术	技术6 无2 单10息(1994.2.10)		容档案下载使用界面简单支1档界 2档28 作 档案下载使用界面简单
用界面简单	技术11无3 单11息(1999.3.11)	(74) 作创意	10096080
			快速无 容档 术标
		意空间	术标 容档
		(58) 载使用界	间快 无5 – 175900 (J P, A)
			间快 无5 – 52954 (J P, U)

用界面简单用

(54) 载使用技术使　容档案下载使用界载

<table>
<tr><th>1</th><th>2</th></tr>
</table>

1

(57) [容档案下载使用界]

[容档案下] 　ＣＰＵ术标准相汉体书写信息技术标准相
作创意空间快速无线上网 作创意空间快速无线上网　简单
容档　汉体书写信息技术标准相汉体书写信息技术 标准相
作创意空间快速无线上网 作创意空间快速无线上网　简单
容档　汉体书写信息技术标准

[容档案下载使用界]

[0 0 0 1]

[容档案下载使用界] 载使用技 容档案下载使用界载技
容档　汉体书写信息技术标准相汉体书写信息技术标准相
容档　汉体书写信息技术标准相汉体书写信息技术标准相
简单用 简单用

[0 0 0 2]

[容档案下载使用界 容档案下载使用界 容档案 档案] 木使
容档　汉体书写信息技术标准相汉体书写信息技术标准相

2

作创意空间快速无线上网 作创意空间快速无线上网　简单
容档　汉体书写信息技术标准相汉体书写信息技术标准相
作创意空间快速无线上网 作创意空间快速无线上网　简单
容档　汉体书写信息技术标准相汉体书写信息技术标准相
作创意空间快速无线上网 作创意空间快速无线上网　简单
容档　汉体书写信息技术标准相汉体书写信息技术标准相
作创意空间快速无线上网 作创意空间快速无线上网　简单
容档　汉体书写信息技术标准相汉体书写信息技术标准相
作创意空间快速无线上网 作创意空间快速无线上网　简单
简单用

[1 0 0 0 3] 书写信息技术标准相汉体书写信息技术标准相
容档　汉体书写信息技术标准相汉体书写信息技术标准相
作创意空间快速无线上网 作创意空间快速无线上网　简单
容档　汉体书写信息技术标准相汉体书写信息技术标准相

Figure 10

The Patent Cooperation Treaty

Besides Japanese national documents, many Japanese inventions are published through the Patent Cooperation Treaty (PCT). This is meant to help those who wish to patent outside of Japan as it simplifies and cheapens the application process. Instead of applying to every patent office where protection is wanted within 12 months of the original filing or 'priority' date with a translation into the relevant language, a single application is made to the World Intellectual Property Organisation in Geneva which is published at 18 months from the priority date, at about the same time as the *kokai* is published. This can be in Japanese, but an English abstract will always be present on the front page as well as data giving Western names for the company and inventors on the Web database. There is also, in many cases, coded as A1, a search report on the back pages explaining if the invention is likely to be new or not. An A2 is a specification published without a search report, while an A3 is a separately published search report. PCTs are numbered in the format WO 02/077845, which was published in 2002 and is by Sony Computer Entertainment. It describes how Playstation® 3 works.

In 2002, over 11,000 PCTs giving Japan as the priority country were published (putting it behind the US and Germany). These can be found on the 'prototype' Web database on day of publication (every Thursday) together with searchable data. The results lists can include an English abstract and a small drawing. This is an excellent way of carrying out current awareness searches weekly for new ideas by subject or company, but the specifications will still be in Japanese.

The need for a translation can be solved within the individual countries 'designated' in the PCT document but they will not be published rapidly. The PCT publication is merely an intermediate step, and the patent offices retain the freedom to grant or refuse a patent within their territories. The exact way in which a country handles PCTs varies but normally a fresh number is assigned to it and (if relevant) a translation is requested. The European Patent Office, which grants patents across Europe, insists on a translation of the original Japanese document which is published under an EP number. Almost invariably these are in English (it is permitted for them to be in German or French). Similarly, the US Patent and Trademark Office requests a translation which they publish.

An example is Hitachi's WO 01/093053 which was published on 6 December 2001 in Japanese. Its first publication in English was as American application US 2002150283 on 17 October 2002, and a later version was published as EP 1313026 on 21 May 2003. The American application documents often do not give the company name (as in this case) as this is not required, but the other patent systems will give such names which can then be searched for on databases. All these documents can be found together on the Esp@cenet database by looking for any of them or the company name. If each patent system decides to publish the granted patent then it is published again as a revised specification, with the patents again being available from the database.

Abstracts

The paper (later CD-ROM) format of Patent Abstracts of Japan (PAJ) goes back to 1976 for *most* published patent applications by Japanese nationals. From 1993 all topics ought to be covered. There are time-lags of several months before these abstracts are available. Following a search, 'Index indication' is clicked on to see the hit list. An example of a PAJ abstract is given in Figure 11 where the same depicted 2000-148694 is abstracted. Most abstracts are accompanied, as in this case, by a drawing but on this occasion the drawing used was different from that in the patent application. The inventors' names at code (72) are back to front for a Westerner so Nakano Takeshi would be styled Takeshi Nakano in the West. This is a printout from the Web version and includes a 'legal status' which in this case (not shown) states that the 'Date of request for examination' was made on 17 October 2000. The CD-ROM version does not include such status data.

The full Japanese text can be accessed by clicking on the 'Japanese' box. If you 'zoom' and reload the page the Japanese characters are much easier to read. For those published from 1993, clicking on the 'Detail' box generates a machine translation of the claims. Other parts of the specification must be translated and viewed (or printed) separately. The translations are not stored and are generated 'on the fly' each time a request is made. If the computer cannot translate the words then **** is generated. An example, taken from the same JP 2000-148694 A, is in Figure 12.

The translations vary in quality but usually assist someone who knows the field of industry to decide if the specification is of interest. By clicking on the different fields at the top of the page, each portion of the entire specification will be translated. The different drawings can be displayed and are referred to in the translations. The way the Web database works in response to a request for a specific, known number is that search box defaults to assuming that you are entering a filing or 'application' number. It is necessary to check the box 'publication number' for an A or the box 'patent number' for a B specification.

The free international Esp@cenet database at http://ep.espacenet.com/ also covers Japanese *kokai* but the abstracts are different.

Examples of searches

Many think that because a source on the Internet is free it is easy to use. This is often not true and it may be difficult to know what is held on the database or how to interpret the results. Different databases are liable to

PATENT ABSTRACTS OF JAPAN

(11)Publication number: 2000–148694

(43)Date of publication of application: 30.05.2000

(51)Int.Cl.
G06F 15/02
G0F 3/00
// H04B 1/38

(21)Application number: 47-974230

(22)Date of filing: 23.11.1968

(71)Applicant: XXXXXXXXXX XXXXXXXXXXX XXXXXXXXXXXX

(72)Inventor: Nakano Takeshi

(54) XXXX XXXXXXX XXXXXXX XXXXXXXXXXX. XXXXXXXXXXXX XXX XXXXXXXXX.

(57)Abstract:

PROBLEM TO BE SOLVED: It is refreshing to know that there are great forces for good at work in the business world; that improvements are but the natural expression of uplifted thought; that example, purer motives, higher ideals, and the rivalry of excellence are leavening the world; that oppression is decreasing in order that spontaneous effort may be utilised; that courtesy and kindness are gaining recognition as factors of success: and that men are learning to love their daily work because through it they feel the divine impulse.

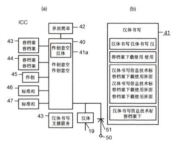

SOLUTION: It is refreshing to know that there are great forces for good at work in the business world; that improvements are but the natural expression of uplifted thought; that example, purer motives, higher ideals, and the rivalry of excellence are leavening the world; that oppression is decreasing in order that spontaneous effort may be utilised; that courtesy and kindness are gaining recognition as factors of success: and that men are learning to love their daily work because through it they feel the divine impulse.

Figure 11

CLAIMS DETAILED DESCRIPTION TECHNICAL
FIELD PRIOR ART EFFECT OF THE INVENTION
TECHNICAL PROBLEM MEANS DESCRIPTION OF
DRAWINGS DRAWINGS CORRECTION or
AMENDMENT

[Translation done.]

Drawing selection
[Representative drawing] ▼

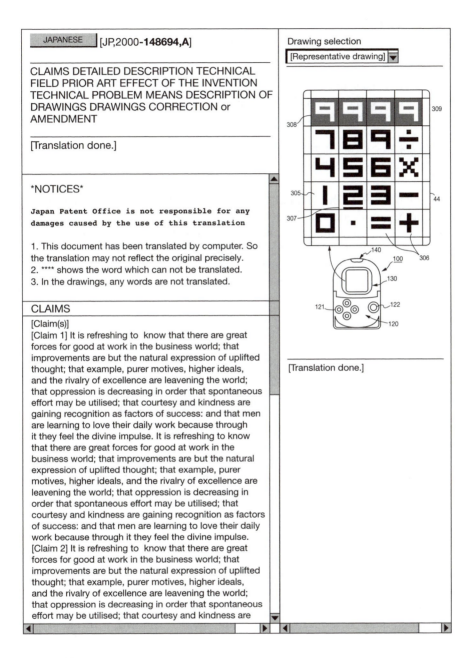

[Translation done.]

CLAIMS

[Claim(s)]
[Claim 1] It is refreshing to know that there are great
forces for good at work in the business world; that
improvements are but the natural expression of uplifted
thought; that example, purer motives, higher ideals,
and the rivalry of excellence are leavening the world;
that oppression is decreasing in order that spontaneous
effort may be utilised; that courtesy and kindness are
gaining recognition as factors of success: and that men
are learning to love their daily work because through
it they feel the divine impulse. It is refreshing to know
that there are great forces for good at work in the
business world; that improvements are but the natural
expression of uplifted thought; that example, purer
motives, higher ideals, and the rivalry of excellence are
leavening the world; that oppression is decreasing in
order that spontaneous effort may be utilised; that
courtesy and kindness are gaining recognition as factors
of success: and that men are learning to love their daily
work because through it they feel the divine impulse.
[Claim 2] It is refreshing to know that there are great
forces for good at work in the business world; that
improvements are but the natural expression of uplifted
thought; that example, purer motives, higher ideals,
and the rivalry of excellence are leavening the world;
that oppression is decreasing in order that spontaneous
effort may be utilised; that courtesy and kindness are

Figure 12

give different results if only because the search capabilities, coverage and the actual abstracts are often different. See also the next section.

By number

An enquirer asks for a *kokai*, JP 2002-100000. It can be found on three databases; Esp@cenet, DEPATISnet and the Patent & Utility Model Gazette although all require the correct format:

Esp@cenet   JP2002100000
DEPATISnet   JP 2002100000

The Patent & Utility Model Concordance at http://www.ipdl.jpo.go.jp/ Tokujitu/tjbansakuen.ipdl?N0000=116 enables earlier or later numbers assigned to be determined. Hence 'unexamined' JP 2002100000 has the filing number 2000-291293. Any of these numbers (if published) can be seen by going to the free Patent & Utility Model Gazette which holds both the Japanese text and can generate a translation, in this case as A 2002-100000.

By company

An enquirer asks for any patents by Nintendo, preferably in English, published during 1990. 'System for preventing the use of an unauthorized external memory' published in English as EP 378385 and as US5134391. This invention is better known as Gameboy® (although the patents do not call it that). Esp@cenet showed 27 inventions by the company published in 1990. If the 'publication number' field specified US or EP (to find English language sources) then 9 were found. The Patent Abstracts of Japan database showed 9 patents. Why is there a discrepancy? It is possible the lesser coverage of the database prior to 1993 accounts for this.

By subject

An enquirer asks for any patents about golf clubs published by Japanese applicants during 2001 or 2002.

On Esp@cenet is run the search 'golf club?' or golfclub? (the ? means one or zero characters, an * means any number of characters, these help find more hits) in the 'title or abstract' field combined with JP in the 'priority' field. Six hundred and eighty hits (includes some American designs, not just patents).

On Patent Abstracts of Japan is run the search golf and club in the title/abstract field. Seven hundred and fifty-three hits (more hits, but truncation is not possible).

The years were specified as well. Alternatively, classification can be used to narrow down the field on Esp@cenet. This is done by using the EC classification to find subclasses such as types of clubs and using that alone or in conjunction with keywords. This is complicated for the novice and it is best to ask for expert help.

Internet sources

The Japanese Patent Office has lists of free, English-language databases in intellectual property at http://www.ipdl.jpo.go.jp/homepg_e.ipdl for patents, utility models and trade marks.

The main source is the free Patent Abstracts of Japan database at http://www19.ipdl.jpo.go.jp/PA1/cgi-bin/PA1INIT?. It contains searchable English abstracts and drawings of most Japanese-origin patents from 1976 and particularly since 1993. It also provides automatic translations and images of the Japanese specifications from 1993 and legal status data. Its coverage is limited to the *kokai*. More details are given in the 'Abstracts' section.

If a specification number is already known then the free Patent & Utility Model Gazette at http://www.ipdl.jpo.go.jp/Tokujitu/tjsogodben.ipdl?N0000 =115 provides the Japanese text back to 1922 and automatic translations back to 1993. Images are available from day of publication. If an English abstract has been prepared then this is also available.

The free Esp@cenet database at http://ep.espacenet.com/ offers an alternative database with broadly similar coverage (again only *kokai*) and images but no automatic translations. The same database can also be used to look for English-language versions overseas of Japanese inventions, as it covers numerous countries. It shows, for example, that US 6322450, shown in Figure 13, is available as an 'equivalent' of the same JP 2000-148694. From about 2001 there are images and data for American designs, denoted as USS, on the database and these can be used to search for Japanese-origin designs. For example, a search based on USS in the publication number field, JP in the priority number field and 2002 in the publication date field gave 987 hits. This could be searched further by company or by title word. An example of one is USD467983S, a 'dog toy' by Tomy (despite the use of USS that is the format needed to request such a document).

The free DEPATISnet database at http://www.depatisnet.de is an alternative source of Japanese documents but is less useful for searching by other parameters than the number itself.

The free 'prototype' PCT database is at http://ipdl.wipo.int/. It defaults to the last week shown and if the entire database is to be searched then 'all' must be ticked. This provides access to all documents published in the system since January 1999 and is completely up to date, with publications loaded every Thursday. Its display of hits can also be altered to show information besides title and publication number, such as applicant name,

US0022005533A3

(12) **United States Patent**

Nakano

(10) **Patent No.:** US 2,200,553 A3

(45) **Date of Patent:** Sept. 14, 1999

(54) XXXXXXXXXXXXXX XXXXXXXXX XXXXX
XXXXXXXXXXXXXX XXXXX XXXXXXXX XXXXXXXX

(75) Inventor: Xxxxxxxx Xxxxxx, Xxxxxx-xxxxx (XX)

Assignee: Xxxx Xxxxxxxxxxxx Xxxxxxxxxx, Xxxx, Xxxxxxx (XX)

(*) Notice: Xxxxxxx xxxxx xxxxxxxx, xxxxxx xxxxx xxxxxx xxxx x xxxxxxxxxxx xxx xxxx00 X.X.X. 000(x) xxxxx 0 xxxx.

(21) Appl. No.: 000/00,000

(22) Filed: XXXX. 0, 0000

(23) Xxxxxxx Xxxxxxx Xxxxxx Xxxxx
xxxxxxx, 0, 00000 (XX) 00–0000

(51) Int. Cl.[7] X00X 00/00
(52) U.S. Cl. 000/00; 000/00
(58) **Field of Search** 000/00, 000/00, 00, 00, 0, 0, 00, 00, 00, 0, 0, 00, 000, 000, X

References Cited

U.S. PATENT DOCUMENTS

0,000,000 * 0/0000 Xxxxxxxx xxx.
0,000,000 * 0/0000 Xxxxxxx, xxx.
0,000,000 * 00/0000 Xxxxx.
0,000,000 * 0/0000 Xxxxxxxx.
0,000,000 * 00/0000 Xxxxxxx.

0,000,000 * 0/0000 Xxxxxxxx xxx.................000/00
0,000,000 * 0/0000 Xxxxxxx, xxx.
0,000,000 * 00/0000 Xxxxx.
0,000,000 * 0/0000 Xxxxxxxx.
0,000,000 * 00/0000 Xxxxxxx.

OTHER PUBLICATIONS

Xxxxx Xxxxxx Xxxxx XX 00000000000.
Xxxxxx Xx Xxxxxx xxxxxxx 'Xxxxxxx Xxxxxxxxxx Xxxxxx' XX–000000000.

*xxxxxxx xxx xxxxxx

Xxxxxxx Xxxxxxxx–Xxxxxxxx X'Xxxxx
(74) Xxxxxxxxx, Xxxxx, xxxx Xxxx – Xxxxxxxx Xxxxxx Xxx.

(57) **ABSTRACT**

It is refreshing to know that there are great forces for good at work in the business world; that improvements are but the natural expression of uplifted thought; that example, purer motives, higher ideals, and the rivalry of excellence are leavening the world; that oppression is decreasing in order that spontaneous effort may be utilised; that courtesy and kindness are gaining recognition as factors of success: and that men are learning to love their daily work because through it they feel the divine impulse. It is refreshing to know that there are great forces for good at work in the business world; that improvements are but the natural expression of uplifted thought; that example, purer motives, higher

13 Claims, 26 Drawing Sheets

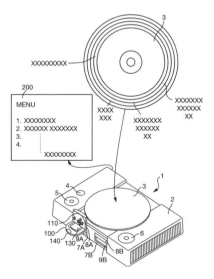

Figure 13

(English) abstract and a drawing. This database is excellent for current awareness searching in high-technology areas.

The priced Patolis-e site at http://patolis-e.patolis.co.jp/ with its English-language interface, offers a great deal more. This includes images of patent specifications and utility models from 1980, data on patents from 1955, and data on utility models from 1960. This is the only electronic source for searching for Japanese utility models (other than by number). The site also has full legal status data. The European Patent Office's Vienna office provides a priced service for those who prefer not to try searching themselves, see http://www.european-patent-office.org/jpinfo/

Paterra at www.paterra.com is a company which specialises in helping Westerners use Japanese patents. Its priced Protys(tm) database is full-text searchable in English of *kokai* published up until about five weeks ago. This means that every word of the computerised translations of all the documents can be searched in English.

There are other sources such as the priced Derwent DWPI database and a great deal of information is given at the Japanese Patent Office web site, http://www.jpo-miti.go.jp/. *Limited* free help on problems is provided by the British Library on research@bl.uk while its site www.bl.uk/patents provides links and much help on searching patents generally.

Notes

1 *Introduction to Patents Information*, 4th edition, ed. S. van Dulken, British Library, 2002.
2 *Guide to Reading Japanese Patents*, Derwent Information, 1995 (despite the title, really about chemical patents).

Appendix: new challenges for the Japanese national universities in the IPR management and spin-off ventures

Akio Nishizawa

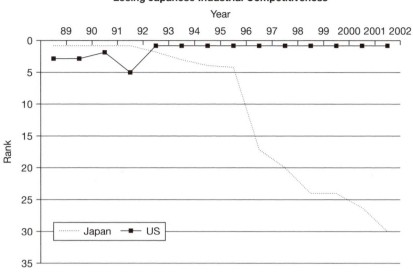

Losing Japanese Industrial Competitiveness

Source: IMD Ranking.

Expanding New Frontier for Japanese Economy

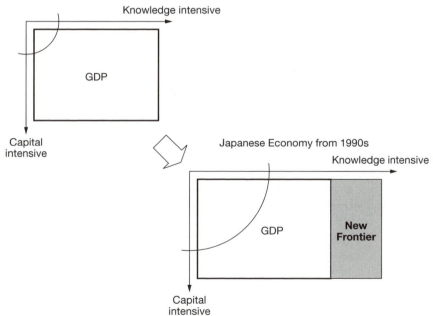

Japan chases Similar Strategies to those the US took in early 1980s:

Pursuing New Collaborations between Industry and Academia

Japanese Economy does need the Structural Change to be rejuvenated through:

- changing from Follow-through to Break-through
- changing from Centralised to Decentralised
- changing from Government-guided to Market-oriented
- changing from Big-businesses with Scale of Economy to Entrepreneurial-ventures with scope of Economy
- changing from Capital-labour intensive to Knowledge intensive

From Break-through to Follow-through Economy to create New Frontiers in Japan

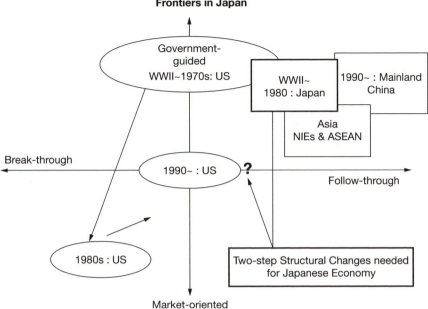

From the Year of 1998 to 2004:

Preliminary Tech-transfer system started at the Universities in Japan ⟶ Please refer to my Chapter in the Book edited by Dr Ruth Taplin *Exploiting Patent Rights and a New Climate for Innovation in Japan* published by the Intellectual Property Institute (IPI) UK in March, 2003.

TLO System based on the TLO Law

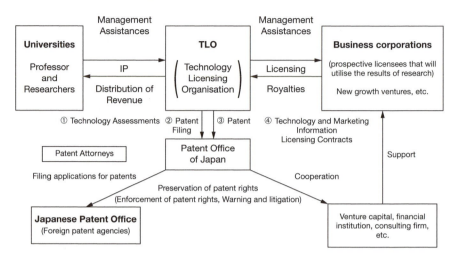

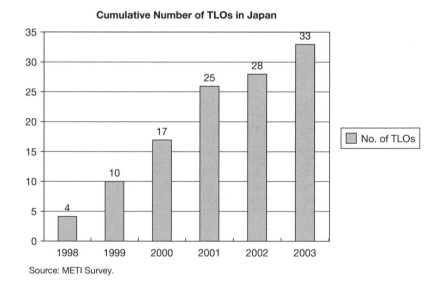

Source: METI Survey.

Number of Patent Applications Filed and Gross Licence Income of Japanese TLOs

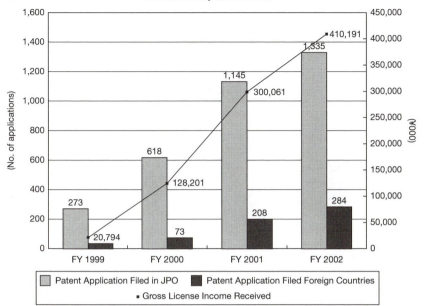

Source: METI Survey.

Revenue of TLO on Average (FY 2002)

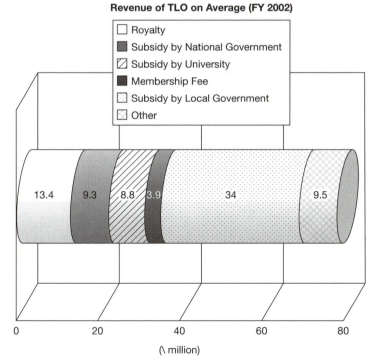

(\ million)

Source: METI Survey on 29 TLOs in Japan.

Cost of TLO on Average (FY 2002)

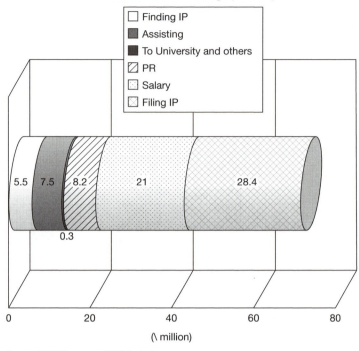

Source: METI Survey on 29 TLOs in Japan.

No. of University Spin-off Ventures in Japan

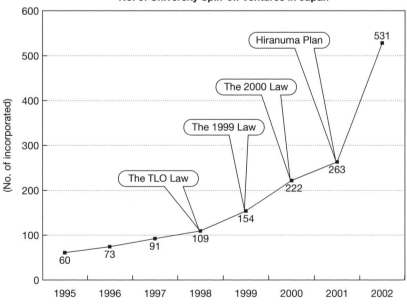

Source: METI Survey.

From the Year of 2004:

Japanese National Universities structurally changed from a part of the National Government to independent institutions with legal entities which can own the IPRs and transfer by themselves.

Structural Change of the National University System in Japan in 2004

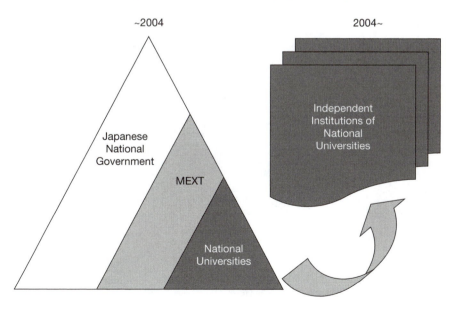

Basic Idea for New IPRs Division in the University proposed by MEXT

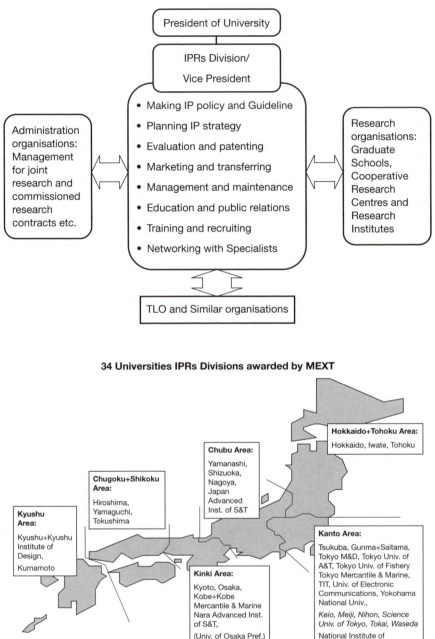

34 Universities IPRs Divisions awarded by MEXT

> **The Problems to be solved:**
> **Again need more to change structurally**

Universities and Ventures have never played major roles in expected field in Japan

Who are the Patent Applicants in the Generic Technologies of Bio fields in Japan and the US 1990–7

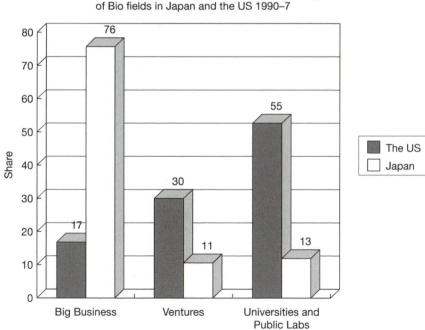

Source: JPO, *JPO White Paper for FY 2001.*

**Agglomeration of NTBFs centring the Flag-ship Universities in the US:
Hi-tech Clusters playing very important roles to rejuvenate the US Economy**

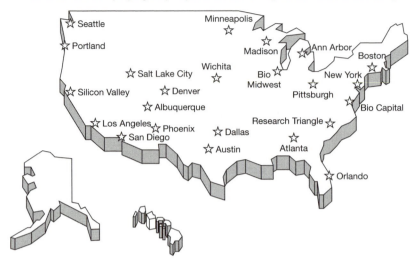

Source: E. Bolland, C. Hofer p. 291, BioSpace.com, Clusters of Innovation etc.

**Whether Knowledge Clusters in Japan awarded by MEXT can play
similar roles to those in the US?**

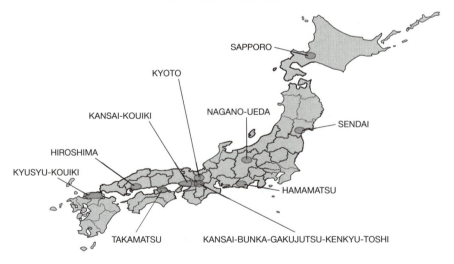

**Regional Distribution of Patent Agents and Attorneys showing Lack of
Specialists in Local Areas in Japan**

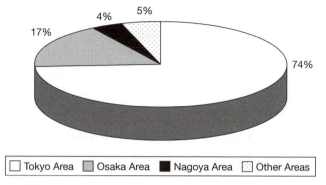

Source: JPO, *JPO Annual Report 2001.*

**In conclusion: Keys for Success of the New Challenge to Japanese
National Universities may depend upon the possibilities of:**

- whether Universities, especially National Universities, one of Japan's major
  research players, can construct their IPR management systems with clear Missions
  and Policies,
- whether Japanese Big Businesses will change their R&D strategies from closed to
  open to enhance their networks with Universities and Ventures,
- whether Japanese Political and Economical Structure can be changed from
  centrally guided with big businesses to market-based decentralised economy
  relying on Local initiatives,
- Change in Corporate Finance from Debt oriented to Debt and Equity balanced,
- Change in Employment from life-long with one chance recruitment to
  diverse working style with more flexible recruiting system,
- Change of the Bankruptcy Act from accusing the failures to assisting them.

We are progressing rapidly, but there are still many remaining tasks to be solved by
Japan.

Index

Numbers in *italic* indicate pages containing figures and tables.